"Didn't even know I was subtexting so often until I read your book. Your examples are teachers. Should be required reading. You've done it again... and again..."

— Alvin Sargent, Academy award-winning screenwriter
Ordinary People; screenwriter *Paper Moon, Spiderman-2, Spiderman-3*

"Linda Seger explores the previously unexplored landscape of subtext in screenwriting in a masterful, intriguing, and insightful way. This book will benefit everyone — professional, aspiring, inquiring, and just plain interested writers. It's a thoroughly good read."

— Syd Field, teacher and author of best-selling book *Screenplay*

"Linda Seger is a born teacher. She has a gift for clarifying the subtleties of language and storytelling, and for offering techniques and insights to writers at all levels. Subtext is a power tool in the writer's arsenal, and following the techniques outlined here could make the difference between good and great. Love the book. Highly recommended!"

— #1 *New York Times* bestselling author Susan Wiggs

"If structure is the skeleton of a screenplay, subtext is its lifeblood. Linda Seger illuminates this vital aspect of the screenwriter's art with the aid of well-chosen examples from dozens of films. The remarks by legendary screenwriter Alvin Sargent make a perfect final chapter, and the filmography at the end is a treasure trove for further study."

— Dan Kleinman, screenwriter: *Rage, Welcome to Oblivion*;
professor of filmmaking at Columbia University

"Seger's *Writing Subtext* reminds the screenwriter — or any writer — to go that extra step to fully examine human interactions and intents and to use what lies beneath the surface to enhance dialogue and action. Using examples from a wide range of films, this book is a great reminder that each word and action can be used in creative and deep ways."

— Jule Selbo, screenwriter: *Hard Promises, Hercules, Young Indiana Jones, Chronicles, Cinderella II* and more; chair of the Radio-TV-Film Department at California State University, Fullerton

"In book after book, Linda Seger gives writers both the tools and the inspiration to transform their work into something truly wonderful. I love this book! Linda brilliantly examines this topic, and has taken it to whole new areas and levels, showing the innumerable ways that carefully chosen dialogue, description, gestures, and images can convey untold layers of meaning and emotion."

— Michael Hauge, script consultant;
author of *Writing Screenplays That Sell* and
Selling Your Story in 60 Seconds

D0036239

"Linda Seger illuminates the power and necessity of subtext in her brilliant new book. A must read for anyone wanting to know the tricks of the trade."

— Linda Purl, actress/founder California
International Theatre Festival

"The power of subtext to intelligently involve your audience cannot be underestimated! In these pages, Linda Seger will give you perspectives and tools to transform good writing into great!"

— Wm. Paul Young, best-selling author, *The Shack*

"Linda's book masterfully deconstructs the art of creating subtext, using numerous excellent examples and helpful exercises. An absolute must for any writer's library!"

— Bill Lundy, The Scriptwriter's Network

"Listen to Linda. Subtext is everything."

— John Truby, author of *The Anatomy of Story*
creator of Blockbuster story software

"Linda Seger is a master of making the intangible tangible. She not only explains the many facets of subtext simply and clearly, using fun and dead-on examples, but she offers user-friendly tricks and exercises to help writers inject subtext into their own work. If you're trying to give your story extra layers, extra depth... or if you've ever run into a wall when thinking about your characters... this book is a godsend."

— Chad Gervich, writer/producer: *Wipeout, Reality Binge, Speeders, Foody Call*; author: *Small Screen, Big Picture: A Writer's Guide to the TV Business*

"*Writing Subtext* take writers to new depths of subtlety and levels of sophistication. Screenwriters should take notice; this book can move your script from 'nice job' to 'greenlight.'"

— Lee Zahavi, product manager, ScriptShark,
http://www.scriptshark.com

writing subtext

WHAT LIES BENEATH

DR. LINDA SEGER

iv

Published by Michael Wiese Productions
12400 Ventura Blvd. #1111
Studio City, CA 91604
tel. 818.379.8799
fax 818.986.3408
mw@mwp.com
www.mwp.com

Cover photo by Edward Nunez
Interior Book Design: Gina Mansfield Design
Editor: Annalisa Zox-Weaver

Printed by McNaughton & Gunn, Inc., Saline, Michigan
Manufactured in the United States of America

Library of Congress Cataloging-in-Publication Data

Seger, Linda.
 Writing subtext : what lies beneath / Linda Seger.
    p. cm.
 Includes filmography.
 ISBN 978-1-932907-96-4
 1. Subtext (Drama, novel, etc.) 2. Motion picture author-
ship. 3. Television authorship. I. Title.
 PN3383.S83S44 2011
 808.2'3--dc22

                          2011002808

Dedicated to the men in my family:
my brother, Fred Seger,
my brother-in-law, Gunther Roth,
my nephew, Greg Anderson,
my grand-nephew, Caleb Austin Stewart (age 4 ½),
and, always to my dear husband, Peter Hazen Le Var

OTHER BOOKS BY LINDA SEGER

Making a Good Script Great

Creating Unforgettable Characters

The Art of Adaptation:
Turning Fact and Fiction into Film

From Script to Screen:
The Collaborative Art of Filmmaking

When Women Call The Shots:
The Developing Power and Influence
of Women in Television and Film

Making a Good Writer Great

Advanced Screenwriting

And the Best Screenplay Goes to:
Learning from the Winners

CONTENTS

ACKNOWLEDGMENTS
ACKNOWLEDGMENTS

Thank you to my readers, who gave me invaluable feedback: Dr. Rachel Ballon, Devorah Cutler-Rubenstein, Cathleen Loeser, Elona Malterre, Kim Peterson, Ellen Sandler, Treva Silverman, and Pamela Jaye Smith.

Thank you to Lucinda Zeising for feedback on Chapter Three.

To my researcher, Lynn Brown Rosenberg, for all of her excellent help.

To Aaron Graham and Alvin Shim — film buffs who helped me with examples and other extras.

To my assistant, Sarah Callbeck, who keeps me organized and always adds a gentle presence to my office.

Thank you to the Michael Wiese team for all their good work — to Michael Wiese and Ken Lee for making it so easy to write, to Annalisa Zox-Weaver for her excellent editing, and to Gina Mansfield, layout artist, for making everything look beautiful.

CHAPTER ONE
CHAPTER ONE

subtext:
a definition and exploration

In drama, more than any other art form, people don't say what they mean. It isn't always a lie. It isn't always fudging or denying the truth. Sometimes characters think they're telling the truth. Sometimes they don't know the truth. Sometimes they don't feel comfortable expressing the truth. In great drama, there are the words themselves and the truth beneath the words. There is the text and the subtext. They are not the same. They're not supposed to be.

WHAT IS TEXT AND SUBTEXT?

Text is the words and gestures that we see. Sometimes they suggest other meanings, and sometimes they just say it like it is. If I asked you, "How do I get from San Francisco to Chicago?" you might answer very clearly, with no subtext: "You take 80 east, and then exit onto Michigan Avenue when you get to Chicago and you'll end up in downtown Chicago." No under-lying meanings there — a nice, straight answer.

But if the question were asked of a cute blonde tart and she answered with a wink, "Why do you want to go to Chicago when there's so much fun to be had here!?" we would know that's not a straight answer. Many other meanings lie beneath the surface. She's promising a good time. She has something else in mind. If you catch her drift, you'll either say, "No, thank you," or decide to stay a while.

We encounter subtext all the time in daily life. People have a habit of not always saying what they mean; or, sometimes they realize that it's not good form, or polite, or acceptable to speak the subtext, so they cover it up with text and let the real meaning simmer beneath the surface. Sometimes they want the other person to understand the real meaning. Sometimes not.

In *The Big Sleep* (1946, by William Faulkner, Leigh Brackett, and Jules Furthman), most of the female characters flirt with Philip Marlowe (Humphrey Bogart). They insinuate, imply, and suggest. Even the female taxi driver has something else in mind besides taking Marlowe to his destination. After she drops him off, she gives him her business card, communicating subtext through her comments.

TAXI DRIVER
If you can use me again sometime,
call this number.

MARLOWE
Day and night?

TAXI DRIVER
Night's better. I work during the day.

Clearly she isn't giving him her card for another taxi ride. Like the cute tart from San Francisco, she has other things on her mind.

Subtext is the true meaning simmering underneath the words and actions. It's the real, unadulterated truth. The text is the tip of the iceberg, but the subtext is everything underneath that bubbles up and informs the text. It's the implicit meaning, rather than the explicit meaning. Great writing and great drama are subterranean. Subtext points to other meanings. The words we hear are meant to lead us to other layers. Conflict exists at this intersection of text and subtext. Great drama dwells beneath the words.

When writers write dialogue that is obvious, we say they're "on-the-nose." Characters say exactly what they mean in neat, logical, sentences. It's dull. It's bland. It sounds like a lecture or a sermon or treatise or a resume. The dialogue is not emotionally alive. The words don't resonate with other meanings. Instead, characters give information, recite backstory and exposition, and comment on unimportant things. They chat, and chat some more.

In obvious dialogue, characters are direct. They are all-knowing and understand everything well enough to explain it all to us. They tell us about their psychological problems — and have self-knowledge and insight and can tell us exactly what's going on. They tell us exactly why they're the way they are, and what childhood forces caused their psychological problems. Nothing is hidden. Like the writer, this character is all-knowing and the writer is determined to have him tell it all.

Or, consider this scene: Two characters meet, and are clearly attracted to each other. They talk about their attraction, about their hopes for the future. They have it all figured out. Everything is out there, without any of the uncertainties or nuances that occur in real life.

When everything is in the text, everything going on is in the lines, not between the lines, as it should be in great writing. It's all there. But what's missing is the important part — the motives and thoughts, emotions and human truths that resonate with multiple meanings.

In *The Great Santini* (1979, by Lewis John Carlino and Herman Raucher from the novel by Pat Conroy), the mother explains

4

to her son, in so many words, the importance of understanding subtext. She says, "You have to learn to interpret the signals he [the father] gives off."

That's what writers need to learn to do: Write subtext so audiences will understand that more is going on than meets the eye. Writers point the way. They choose suggestive words and describe revealing behavior so that audiences get a whole lot more information than they could ever get from just a line of dialogue.

HOW DO WE KNOW THERE'S SUBTEXT?

Subtext is all the meanings that are not stated, but lie beneath. It's what's really going on. What the movie is really about. In this book, I use a fairly broad definition of subtext because what lies beneath is not just beneath the words: Subtext can be found beneath words, gestures, behaviors, actions, and images.

Usually subtext is something you can't quite put your finger on. It is felt. You sense it. We know we're encountering subtext because of the feelings of uncertainty we have and the questions we might ask. We encounter subtext when we wonder: "Hmmm, that doesn't seem quite right. What did the person really mean?" Or, we think, "Yeah, sure, I just don't believe a word of it!" Or, we feel uneasy, and sense, "I'm sure there's more going on here than it seems. I wonder what he's up to, and why is he doing that?"

In her book *The Film Director's Intuition*, directing and acting coach Judith Weston explains:

> Language is what we say with our words, and subtext is what we really say, with our body language, with the tone of our voice, with our eyes and expression. Subtext expresses our real feelings — for instance, feelings of impatience or distaste which may lurk beneath small talk and compulsory politeness. Subtext is the emotional history, intention, metaphor, and emotional event at the center of the scene.

Subtext adds depth. Judith adds, "Without subtext, the movie   5
can be superficial."

EXPRESSING SUBTEXT

You can express subtext in a number of ways. You might have
the text say one thing and have the subtext say the opposite.
Suppose you ask your friend, "How are you?" and he replies,
"Fine, very well, thank you," as he packs up his belongings to
leave the office, having just been fired. If you found out the real
situation, you would know the subtext: He means the opposite
of what he says.

Sometimes subtext implies multiple meanings and allows several possible interpretations. If someone says, "I'm going away.
I just can't take it anymore," you might wonder: Is she taking a
weekend off? Just going away? Is she going to kill herself? And
what is the "it" she can't take anymore? How bad is "it"? Is this
behavior related to the fact her husband left her, or because
they went bankrupt, or because her son is on drugs? So you
start thinking of all sorts of associations and possibilities and
interpretations. You don't know for sure what's going on, but
you do know something is. And, if you know there's subtext,
you might recognize the danger and decide to ask a few questions of your friend. Perhaps you go with her for the weekend
to make sure she's not alone. Maybe you suggest that she not
take the gun.

Even if we recognize subtext, its true meaning might be known
to the character but unknown to everyone else. It's the character's secret, those little problems and flaws that only he or she
understands but doesn't want others to know about.

Or, the subtext might be invisible even to the character, and
reside deep within the unconscious but affect the character's
actions, emotions, and choices. Sometimes the subtext is also
invisible to the writer, who discovers it in the process of writing.
Eventually, the audience needs to know, sense, or be aware of
the truth, without anyone explaining it directly.

6

Subtext is not just the meanings beneath the words, but it is also the associations we bring to dialogue and images. You, as the writer, choose the words in both dialogue and description that resonate most. But you also must consider actions and emotions and gestures and images, not just lines of dialogue. A sunset might provoke associations of romance, of the end of things as night and darkness come, of nostalgia for what might have been, of the possibility of new events taking place in the secret, romantic night. A sunset has become a cliché because we bring so many associations to this image. We have seen it so often in films. A film just has to show a sunset and we usually know everything it means. It is a tired subtext, greatly over-used. But, it is subtextual, nevertheless, because we don't just take it at face value. We know it means a great deal more than the end of the day.

Always, with subtext, we know something more is going on. Something is unspoken – something that, if written well, is drama at its very best.

REAL-LIFE SUBTEXT

Dramatic subtext is based on our own experiences and our understandings of how people tick. As writers and artists, we watch people in real life and then use our accrued understanding to create dramatic, dynamic characters. We learn what people hide and what they choose to reveal. We learn how people don't mean what they say or say what they mean and how much figuring out we have to do to learn what's really going on. We recall richly layered scenes from our own lives, and examine them for subtext. We may recognize that, in real life, subtext often wastes our time and muddies our relationships because we're forced to spend so much time figuring out what's really going on. We try to fathom what's up and keep thinking: "Something's wrong here, but I don't know what it is!"

Although we think we'd prefer that people be direct with us, and many of us learn to be direct with others (usually through years of therapy), plenty of subtext still goes on in our real-life words. When the cute new guy you met doesn't call (although he said he would), you don't know if that means he really isn't interested, he's out of town, he's lying in a hospital, or he's dead. When the cute guy finally calls, and you ask him if he wants to come to your apartment for coffee, you know – and he knows – it's not about coffee.

Psychotherapist and script consultant Dr. Rachel Ballon says, "Dating is subtext, marriage is text." And this arrangement is often the case. In the first months of a courtship, we often don't know what anything means and whether we can trust the words, or what's really going on and what it means for our future. Everything seems to be about interpretation, and we often get the subtext wrong.

In marriage, we hope that most communication is out in the open, truthful and clear, although there are plenty of marriages with too much subtext – with secrets, hidden meanings, and emotions that rumble, but go unspoken.

Dr. Ballon also says that, as children, we start our lives with text, but then learn subtext as we come to understand social behavior, social norms, what is acceptable and what is not. Children will usually be quite direct, until adults move their text into subtext so they become more "socially appropriate." Perhaps the child meets Aunt Jeannie and screams, "I don't want to kiss her. She's ugly." The parents are appalled, embarrassed, and quickly teach the child to shy away from the text. The child learns to say, "Hello, Aunt Jeannie. I have a cold, so I can't kiss you hello." The child is learning to hide the text in the subtext, so the text, the real meaning, moves to the subtext.

If someone says, "I always hated Sunday dinners with the family," we know there is subtext. If we have the time, we might ask, "Why?" "Was this a time of arguments and conflict in the family? Did the father get drunk at Sunday dinner? Did the mother always cry because the weekend had gone badly?"

8

Or, you might hear your friend say, "We fell in love instantly. It was clearly love at first sight. We are soul-mates!" However, you are a bit suspicious because she's clinging to the arm of her new boyfriend, has fallen in love instantly a number of times, and the new man in her life reminds you of her father.

Or, you might have heard a president or dictator say, "We're going to war for the cause of freedom!" Maybe. But upon closer examination, you notice the enemy has vast oil fields or vast rubber plantations or other rich resources that will become the booty of war. Or, you notice this ruler has gone to war a number of times and freedom has not been the result.

Sometimes the aspiring suitor says to the lovely young woman at dinner, "You can have anything you want. My treat." But when she orders the expensive steak, the frown on his face and his cool behavior to her during the meal clearly indicate that she has crossed a line and that her excess bothers him.

Sometimes one friend says to another, "It's really fine for you to go out with my former boyfriend. No problem!" Well, maybe, maybe not. If there's subtext, this action will have repercussions.

We might think subtext more often occurs in professional relationships or new love relationships — places where not everything can be expressed outright. But even friends don't always tell us the truth. When you ask, "Does this dress make me look fat?" there are many ways to answer the question — some with subtext, some without. The friend might answer with straight text: "Yes, but only around the waist, and just a bit around the hips. And your butt does stick out a bit more than it does with your other clothes. Otherwise, it's a nice color."

Or, the friend might answer, "No, it's fine. It's a pretty dress!" And you might think, "What does that mean?" Now you're unsure whether to buy the dress or not. You notice that the friend didn't say, "You look stunning in it. It becomes you. Wow — they'll be lining up around the block if you wear something so smashing!" But, maybe your friend is telling the truth, and it is pretty so you decide to buy the dress. The answer seems very straight, without subtext. And maybe it is. But you do worry about that word "fine."

Or, you might try to guess the subtext. Perhaps the friend is secretly thinking, "I wish I could look that good. Great taste. I wish I had some of that!" And jealousy has now reared its green-eyed head. Or, the attractive platonic friend whom you always thought was "just a friend" suddenly seems to be looking at you in a funny and unfamiliar way. The friend might really think, "You are a feast to the eyes. I've never seen you look so attractive. Actually, you're gorgeous and I'm very interested!" The friend might suggest you shouldn't buy the dress after all, because you're far too much of a babe magnet in it and the friend doesn't want you attracting anyone else. If this interpretation is the subtext, the friend might say, "It's too expensive," or "Well, maybe it's not as becoming as this other one." Now you're really confused.

When you're confused, you are probably experiencing subtext. Something is going on underneath the surface. You don't know what, for sure. You don't know where it will lead. You don't know what else will bubble up and what will remain hidden. But something is nagging at you and you think there might be some conflict here, perhaps a bit of trouble in this relationship, or maybe a turn in some new and wonderful direction. Perhaps something that's been percolating in your hidden thoughts will come out as you find there's a mutual attraction. Maybe you were implying subtext also.

Perhaps you put on the dress to test the friend and see if something else could go on between the two of you. Or maybe you put on the dress to let the friend know you now are interested in someone else and you're getting ready to go to a fancy restaurant — with the cute guy you met last week.

Either way, the characters are becoming layered. Now there's subtext.

CONSCIOUS SUBTEXT

In some instances, people are aware of their own subtext but choose not to share it with others. This discretion can take place in an attraction between people, when one chooses not to let the other know his or her true feelings. This might happen because the one person feels it's too soon to express true feelings, or that it's inappropriate to express feelings because the other person is married, is the boss, is too old, too young, too rich, too poor, too educated, or not educated enough, or from an undesirable culture, whatever that might mean to close friends or relatives. So the subtext comes out in other ways — looks between the two, comments like, "Your hair looks pretty," or "Cool car," when the person really means "You're pretty, I like you," or "You're cool, even cooler than your car!"

The Romeos and Juliets can't publicly say what they really feel. They know what they think and feel, but they direct their words and actions so others won't understand them.

UNCONSCIOUS SUBTEXT

Sometimes subtext is unknown to a person because it's too painful, too shameful, too dishonorable, or too difficult to admit. People who have suffered from abuse as small children, perhaps incest, battering, or neglect, often do not remember the very incidents that inform much of their lives. The woman might not know why she is afraid of the uncle or why she pushes her boyfriend away when he becomes romantic. The man might not know that he's uncomfortable with the affections of a woman because he has repressed childhood abuse that occurred with a female relative. After years of therapy, perhaps the unconscious becomes conscious and the hidden layers of life become known well enough to make clear pronouncements and decisions.

Of course we all have flaws, insecurities, some problems, but for some, these problems have left deep wounds, some of them unconscious. Traumatic incidents from childhood might cause a character to speak, act, and react in ways that seem abnormal, or that imply the character is hiding something. In the film *Sybil* (1976), based on the book about a woman with multiple personalities, the backstory eventually emerges, as we learn that Sybil's mother abused her as a child and her father ignored all the signs. Throughout the film, Sybil's fears often erupt, causing her to have strong reactions to simple stimuli, such as being on the street. Simple stimuli provoke strange behavior, such as climbing to the top of a bookcase when she gets scared. Likewise, simple affection from the sweet man next door causes her to recoil, yet, she has no idea why. Through work with a therapist, these underlying psychological traumas emerge. She learns that these extreme reactions are caused by traumas from early childhood.

Other movies about multiple personalities, such as *The Three Faces of Eve* (1957), or films about mental illness or other psychological problems, such as *I Never Promised You a Rose Garden* (1977), *David and Lisa,* (1962), *I'm Dancing as Fast as I Can,* (1982), *One Flew Over the Cuckoo's Nest* (1975), *Frances* (1982), *Girl, Interrupted* (1999), *A Beautiful Mind* (2001), *Don't Say a Word* (2001), and *The Soloist* (2009), tell stories about rooting out unconscious problems, which are able to heal as they become conscious.

A bad break-up, bad luck with relationships, or unresolved relational problems in the past can cause someone to be unable to love or to become averse to being involved with or committed to someone (*Up in the Air* [2009], *Runaway Bride* [1999], *High*

12

Fidelity [2000], *500 Days of Summer* [2009], *My Fair Lady* [1964]).
The excuse might be "I'm too busy," or "I don't think we're
right for each other," or "I just met someone else," but the real
truth may be under the surface. Perhaps the person is really
trying to say: "I'm still not over my last relationship but I don't
want to talk about it with someone I've just met," or "I don't
want to get close to anyone after the pain of the last break-up,
but that makes me sound weak so I'm not going to allow myself
to be vulnerable with you by discussing this."

Subtext can be expressed through the emotions of a character
— either by displaying the emotion or by hiding it. Sometimes
characters feel their emotional reactions are not appropriate
and therefore have to be suppressed; but then the emotions
come out in some other way. In the comedy *Broadcast News* (1987,
by James Brooks), broadcast journalist Jane Craig (Holly Hunter)
tries to keep her professional persona intact, but certain unconscious problems and motivations come through. Jane has a
crying spell every morning in her apartment because a woman
of her professional caliber is not supposed to cry at the office.
At work, she keeps her "I've-got-it-all-together" persona in
place, even though it's clear to the audience that she doesn't
have it all together.

Jane is jealous of a male colleague's developing affections for
another woman on their team. Because emotions such as jealousy are not considered appropriate between two professional
women (so some say), Jane hides her emotions, but uses her
authority to send her female colleague on an assignment to
distant cold Alaska. Either way, the audience understands the
motivations in the subtext.

Desires, dreams, and wishes can also inform subtext. Some
desires we do not dare share. You might want your script to
get sold to Steven Spielberg and become a huge box office hit,
but you feel that's unrealistic and silly, so you don't let anyone
know how you've conspired to meet him. You have rehearsed,
innumerable times, what you'll say at the exact moment your

paths cross and, although you plan to tell your friends after it's all over, right now, you act blasé about everything to do with your script. Your dreams seem much too big to share at this time, even with friends.

Subtext may motivate many of our normal activities. You might not know why you're driven to sell a script, earn a college degree, buy a red sports car, or sign up for the Army to fight in a war. Of course, all of these actions can be motivated for good, solid, conscious reasons. But not always. If you're obsessed with a particular effort, and things seem out of proportion in terms of how you are going about fulfilling a goal, subtext might explain your motivation. Perhaps you realize, after some consideration of the obsession, that it's all about getting daddy's approval, about making up for a deprived childhood, wanting the high school kids to know you made it after all, or wanting to get your name in the newspaper because when you were ten you won second place in the community talent show and there was a big fuss made about you and you had your name in the newspaper and everyone talked nicely about you. That experience motivated your desire for approval all your life – and, besides, all along, you felt you should have come in first.

Whatever the reason, you can sense there's something else going on that bothers you and pushes at you and doesn't let up. And if you put this subtext into your character, the audience will feel it too.

SUBTEXT THROUGH IMPLIED SEXUALITY

Sometimes a film doesn't want to make explicit statements about the sexuality of its characters, especially if they partake in what might be considered abnormal behavior. In *Lolita* (1962), Humbert Humbert is clearly interested in the adolescent Lolita, although he pretends to be in love with her mother. Innuendos signal his interest, including his concern that Lolita might

14

be going out too much, which is really a concern he'll have to spend too much time with the clinging, seductive mother while waiting for Lolita to come home.

If they are gay, depending on the context, characters may experience struggles accepting their sexuality. *Brokeback Mountain* (2005), which begins its story in 1963, gives a fairly clear portrayal of two gay men surviving in the face of society's attitudes toward homosexuality by acting straight. The night after the two men first make love, Ennis states, "I'm not gay," which is belied by his emotions and actions.

Sometimes the relationship between two people is deliberately left ambiguous, and the subtext merely implies a relationship, or strongly suggests one (*Women in Love* [1969], *Troy* [2004], *Brideshead Revisited* [2008]).

In *Bonnie and Clyde* (1967, by David Newman and Robert Benton), the sexual subtext differs between the script and the film, partly because of the casting. In the script, Clyde is in his early 20s. Bonnie is also very young, but sexually much more aggressive. In spite of her willingness (and in spite of the fact they sleep in the same bed), their relationship isn't consummated. Often C. W. is sleeping in the same room, or Clyde doesn't seem interested in being alone, or he shifts the focus as soon as they start making out. We might ask, "What is Clyde's problem? Is this a moral problem?" which would seem odd, considering that he shoots guns with lots of bullets, and doesn't seem to have a problem crossing other moral boundaries. Toward the end of the script, Bonnie reads him her poem about "Bonnie and Clyde," which tells their story and characterizes him as a notorious criminal. This recognition galvanizes a new image of him, as Clyde realizes he has "made it" and achieved his goals.

The description in the script clarifies the subtext we have probably sensed throughout: "It is all starting to come out now — his realization that he has made it, that he is the stuff of legend, that he is an important figure!"

No hero is complete without the conquest of the damsel, so he
finally makes love to Bonnie. In the script, after they make love,
Clyde reacts, clearly pleased with himself:

```
              CLYDE
(chuckling, apparently quite pleased.)
        Damn!... damn... damn!
```

As Clyde looks at Bonnie for some kind of approval, the stage directions mention his "underlying anxiety," which is beginning to
surface.

```
              CLYDE
Hey, listen, Bonnie, how do you feel?...


              BONNIE
              Fine.


              CLYDE
I mean you feel like you're s'posed
    to feel after you've uh...
```

His hesitance implies his unsurety. He desperately wants her
approval.

```
    Well, that's good, ain't it. Reason I ask
Is, I uh... Well, I figger it's a good idea to ask. I
    mean how else do I tell if I did it the way...


              BONNIE
    ... Hey. You done just perfect.


              CLYDE
    I did, didn't I? I mean I did, I really did.
    I did it, I did, I mean this as my first time
        and it was just like rollin' off a log.
When it comes right down to it, it was easy, I mean I didn't
              even have to try.
```

So, now the subtext became clear: Clyde was unsure and afraid
that he wouldn't be able to do it right for Bonnie. Clyde, in the
script, is a virgin.

16 The film shifts this subtext. Warren Beatty and Faye Dunaway look older than early 20s, so there seem to be other reasons for the lack of sexual activity between them. It is clear throughout the script that Bonnie is frustrated by Clyde's lack of sexual response. After he robs the grocery store, their first robbery together, they hole up in a house out of town. Bonnie sleeps inside and Clyde sleeps out by the car. Immediately, we might wonder why. Over and over again, Clyde will start making out with Bonnie, and then stop.

At various times in the film, Clyde makes comments about his sexuality. Shortly after they meet, as they start to make out and it's clear that Bonnie is eager and willing, Clyde tells her:

> CLYDE
> I ain't much of a lover boy...
> Ain't nothing wrong with me, I don't like boys...

Later, he tells her:

> CLYDE
> If all you want is a stud service
> you get on back to West Dallas and you stay
> there the rest of your life.... You could
> find a lover boy on every damn corner in town.

Out of Bonnie's frustration, she accuses him:

> BONNIE
> Your advertising is just dandy.
> Folks never guess you don't have a thing
> to sell.

Bonnie wants to be alone with Clyde, but over and over again, he makes sure they aren't. C. W. is around and so is Buck, his brother. Bonnie tells him:

> BONNIE
> Always somebody in the next room... Don't
> you just want to be alone with me?

> CLYDE
> I always feel like we're alone.

>   BONNIE
>   Do you, baby?

Then Clyde changes the subject:

>   CLYDE
>   I'm hungry.

Later, Bonnie tells him outright:

>   BONNIE
>   The only special thing about
> you is your peculiar ideas about love-
> making which is no lovemaking at all!

Although ambiguity surrounds Clyde in the film version, several viewers I spoke to reached the conclusion that he is impotent until Bonnie writes the "Bonnie and Clyde" poem. Then he feels like he's finally somebody.

>   CLYDE
>   You told my story.
>   One time I told you I was gonna
>   make you somebody, that's what
>   you done for me!

After they make love, they seem to have finally come together as a couple in love. Clyde expresses tenderness and Bonnie shows obvious satisfaction. He still expresses uncertainty, but the motivation for this sexual ambiguity is not because it was his first time, as in the script:

>   CLYDE
>   Hey, how you feel? I mean you feel
>   like you're supposed to feel
>   after you... ?

>   BONNIE
>   You did just perfect.

>   CLYDE
>   I did, didn't I?

It's not unusual for sexual information about a character to be hidden in the subtext, as it is in *Bonnie and Clyde*. The truth usually comes out with more clarity later in the story. This information still needs to be implied so we can begin to guess about what is going on. It's layered throughout — a little here, a little there. Another hint here. A bit of nuance there.

In *Thelma and Louise* (1991, by Callie Khourie), Louise reacts with rage to Harlan's attempted rape — she kills him. As the story goes on, we get hints that Louise was raped in Texas some time before, and that clearly justice had not been served. Before shooting Harlan, she tells him that when someone is crying, she's not having any fun. When she tells Thelma that she'll head to Mexico, she also explains that she won't go through Texas. She says, "I'm not talking about it." She understands a great deal about how the law works, and about the lack of evidence to indicate that the killing was done in self-defense. She understands the deep trouble they're in. Finally, Thelma mentions the word "rape," as she clearly adds up the subtext:

THELMA
It happened to you, didn't it?...
You was raped!

As the story proceeds, even the detective is clear about what happened, and feels sympathy for both women.

Just as underlying sexual problems can be in the subtext, so too can underlying attraction. True, most of the time the attraction between two people is fairly clear — to them and to the audience. It's in the text. But, sometimes it's in the subtext. Perhaps two characters seem to dislike each other, but we know that they're truly attracted to each other. Maybe there's an underlying conflict, but we know it's really because there's so much electricity between them.

Or, sometimes the attraction is clear, but it's expressed in both the text and the subtext. Sometimes we sense the meaning of the subtext in a scene between two attractive people, even though they're talking about everything *but* their attraction to each other. In *Up in the Air* (2009), the initial flirtation consists of two people showing each other their credit cards in their wallets, a scene suggestive of "You show me yours, I'll show you mine."

In many James Bond films, the initial meeting, as well as some of the repartee in other get-togethers, clearly contains subtext. In the remake of *Casino Royale* (2006, by Neil Purvis, Robert Wade, and Paul Haggis), James Bond meets Vesper Lynd in the dining car of the train. She's attractive (of course) and has been assigned to work with him and be the money source so he can take part in a high-stakes poker game. The scene moves between text and subtext, with James Bond usually lacing his lines with subtext. I've inserted the subtext throughout the scene, which begins as she joins him at his table:

```
                    VESPER
              I'm the money.
```

Note: This is a straight statement. It seems to be text without subtext. She's stating the reason for their meeting, but the text is still slightly provocative. She doesn't say "I'm in charge of the money," but "I'm the money," which is more personal and gives Bond entry into the subtext.

```
                     BOND
              Every penny of it.
```

James immediately turns the scene into subtext. Yes, she looks like a million — every inch of her. He clearly is attracted.

```
                    VESPER
        The Treasury has agreed to stake you
                 in the game.
```

Vesper now moves back to the text. This is why she's here — to explain these details. She tries to be no-nonsense, to-the-point, but it isn't going to work with James. She hands him her business card, which re-emphasizes the text of the scene.

BOND
                                (examining the card)
                            Vesper? I hope you gave your
                                parents hell for that.

James won't stick to the text. He starts with text, noticing her name, but immediately begins to imply subtext. He first implies there's something wrong with her name. He's implying, "Who would want to be saddled with the name Vesper?" But the writer, in this case, Ian Fleming, has chosen the name, partly for its subtextual meaning. What does "vesper" mean? It implies evening, which can be filled with possibilities. In the Catholic Church, vespers is the evening service, although we can be reasonably sure James has nothing religious in mind when he examines Vesper. Vespers can imply twilight, a time when things aren't always seen clearly, or are meant to be secret. It's an evocative name.

Vesper continues to speak the text — ten million dollars was wired to his account and he can get five million more if necessary. She asks about the menu and they begin to eat. As the meal proceeds, Vesper is clearly not convinced that James can be trusted to win at poker. She's not sure their money is in good hands. Bond tries to show he knows the game well.

                                    BOND
            ... in poker you don't play your hand, you play the
                            man across from you.

Bond continues to show his knowledge, giving her information in the text, while trying to convince her of his abilities in the subtext.

                                   VESPER
                    And you're good at reading people.

It sounds as if Vesper is doing straight text, but Bond catches the subtext.

          BOND
    Which is why I've been able to
  detect the undercurrent of sarcasm
        in your voice.

Now Bond is saying outright that he has understood the subtext all along — he understands she doesn't trust him.

         VESPER
  I am now assured our money is in
       good hands.

         BOND
  From which one might surmise you
  aren't overwhelmingly supportive
     of this plan of action.

Bond is now reading another subtext here — it isn't just about distrust of him, but distrust of the whole plan. We might not have understood the subtext, but he did — because he's good at reading people. In case we missed it, he explains the subtext to us very clearly.

         VESPER
  So there is a plan? Excellent.
  Somehow I got the impression we
  were risking ten million dollars
  and hundreds of people's lives on a
 game of luck. What else can you surmise?

The sarcasm is there, but now something else is coming out. If Vesper wanted to keep this business-like, she wouldn't be engaging him by asking a personal question. We might think she's still talking about the plan, but most likely not. She is probably asking him to surmise something personal. She must admit she's attracted also. And, as we can see from her last comments at the end of the scene, she has noticed all along he's an attractive and charming fellow.

         BOND
    About you?

22   He got the subtext of her question, and puts it into the text; he
studies her, enjoying this turn in the conversation.

> Well, your beauty is a problem.
> You worry that you won't be taken
> seriously... ???

Now, the whole conversation becomes personal. He guesses
that she overcompensates for her beauty with her clothes, that
she uses arrogance to compensate for her insecurity, and that
she's an only child or an orphan. She guesses he went to Oxford
and didn't have money, and that he is also an orphan. Then she
zings him once more:

> VESPER
> ... you think of women as
> disposable pleasures rather than
> meaningful pursuits, so as charming
> as you are,

Ah, she noticed!

> I will be keeping my
> eye on our government's money and
> off your perfectly formed ass.

> BOND
> You noticed.

Yes, we got the subtext also. She noticed. She's attracted, but
doesn't want him to get the better of her. She asks:

> VESPER
> ... How was your lamb?

> BOND
> Skewered. One sympathizes.

She did get the better of him, and he knows it. Of course, as
the film continues, Bond will fall deeply in love with her and

won't treat her as a disposable pleasure but rather will see her as a meaningful pursuit.

LOOK FOR THE SUBTEXT AT CRISIS POINTS

Subtext is most apt to come through during crisis or at transition points in our lives — when a death occurs, a new job is taken, at the start of a new relationship or the break-up of an old one — when the stakes are high and everything might rest on our saying and doing the right thing — even though we're not sure what the "right thing" is. In such cases, characters cover up the real meanings.

In any kind of suffering, a myriad of emotions often leaves one speechless, so the subtext may be expressed visually, rather than verbally. Most people have difficulty facing pain, or knowing what to do when confronted with the unfamiliar. They might become stoic, denying their feelings and discomfort. They don't want others to know how vulnerable they are.

When people are ashamed, they can't speak about it. They want respect but may fear that they'll lose it if others know the truth. What do they talk about instead? Perhaps nothing at all; or, perhaps they become overly polite in their relationships with colleagues; or, perhaps they turn to discussions about the weather, information about their job, or polite inquiries about their colleague's family. Even when writing this dialogue, words can be carefully chosen to imply what is really being said: "I want your respect. I'm going to gain it by politeness to make you think I'm a kind person, or by the knowledge I share to make you think I'm a smart person."

When a friend or parent lays dying, knowing how direct one can be (so the subject of death might be skirted) can be difficult. Every subject is discussed except death. The son might go on and on about who won the football game, but is really talking about whether the father will be able to win the battle between

24   life and death. The daughter might be trying to make the
father comfortable or might be smoothing the blanket on his
bed, even though he's taking his last breath and such neatness
really doesn't matter anymore. The sister might feel helpless
and uncomfortable, wanting to get out of there, and so quickly
volunteers to go get the nurse. Immediately, the brother simply
says, "Well, that's that!" And it is. But even those words imply
vulnerability, discomfort, and perhaps a desire to get back to
life. Enough of this death stuff!

In the script of *Remains of the Day* (1993, by Ruth Prawer Jhabvala),
when he is dying, Stevens Sr. says to his son, Stevens:

> FATHER
> I hope I've been a good father to you.

And Stevens, who is always dignified and unemotional, changes
the subject:

> STEVENS
> I'm glad you're feeling better. I have
> to go down now. A lot to see to.

The father tries again.

> FATHER
> I'm proud of you. I hope I've been
> a good father to you.

Stevens ignores the subject again.

> STEVENS
> I have so much to do, Father, but
> we'll talk again in the morning.

Then the father decides to tell him another truth — about the
mother.

```
                        FATHER
           I fell out of love with your mother.
            Your mother was a bitch. I loved
            her once but love went out of me
          when I found out what a bitch she was.
              Your mother was a bitch.
```

Once more, Stevens ignores the emotional truth.

```
                       STEVENS
            I'm glad you're feeling better.
```

Even when Miss Kenton informs Mr. Stevens that his father passed away, all Stevens can say is: "Oh, I see."

CULTURAL SUBTEXT

Those of us who travel to other countries often notice that sometimes we simply don't know what's going on. This confusion might not be because we don't know the language, but because we don't know cultural meanings that are hidden to someone of another culture. Physical proximity changes from one culture to another. We might not know how to interpret the person standing very near to us — attraction? Is the person a pickpocket? A sex pervert? Or, is this nearness part of a culture that is simply used to people standing close to each other?

Some cultures don't like to say "no." After I had been invited to give a seminar in Japan, I didn't hear from my host for many weeks. Believing this lack of response might be cultural, and that he might not be able to do the seminar, I read a book about Americans doing business with Japan and discovered that the Japanese don't like to say "no," so they often find other ways to say "no" without ever saying it, such as by not responding. After reading the book, I was even more confused, because I had no idea whether my host was trying to say "no," or whether something else was wrong. Was there subtext, or not? Since there had been no reply to my emails, I finally faxed him. I received a fax back saying he had changed his email address and still wanted me to come.

A friend who just returned from Taiwan said he had to learn not to complain, even when he was served "old" tea that tasted terrible. He learned that complaining was not appropriate in that culture because it was taken as an insult.

Some cultures have subtext around gift-giving, or around hospitality. In Ecuador, it's considered polite to have a drink with whomever you're meeting, even if you just stopped to ask directions to the nearest village or volcano. Typically the drink is locally brewed alcohol so you have to watch it, lest you won't be able to wobble down the street and actually make it to your destination. The subtext seems to be about accepting people and their hospitality; to refuse would be a social snub and a personal slight.

In the Philippines, you have to be careful about saying you admire something. Typically your host or friends will simply give it to you or buy it for you. That idea can work very nicely when you're on the receiving end, but it works both ways. There can be a tendency to ask you for favors and things you might not be comfortable doing, parting with, or buying. If you don't understand the subtext, you won't understand what you're supposed to do in return.

Cultures vary in terms of what is acceptable with nudity. Some tourists go to beaches in foreign countries and their eyes pop out, as they notice naked men and women on the beach. No big deal! In other cultures, exposing the neck, ankles, arms, or knees is not acceptable. The subtext comes through the reactions of others. Wearing a sleeveless blouse in some Middle Eastern cultures that frown on such exposure might seem fine because it's warm, but the looks and frowns from others may soon alert you that it's time to go back to the hotel and change. This tradition can also hold in Muslim countries, such as some parts of Indonesia and Malaysia, where spare sarongs at the entrance to temples indicate that any females in shorts or slacks should use one to cover up while in the temple. They can also be used as a shawl to cover bare shoulders. It's similar to the up-scale restaurant that supplies suit jackets and ties for men who don't seem to know how to dress appropriately.

In The Old West, asking a man where he came from was not appropriate. The past was private. You didn't ask personal questions. In the film *Shane* (1953), we never know where Shane comes from, or where he is going to, but the audience knows that something is hidden and secret in his past. Nothing needs to be said — it's clear.

Hollywood has its own cultural context. If someone says to you, "Don't call us, we'll call you!" and you wait by the phone for weeks, you clearly didn't understand the subtext, which was, in most cases, "Not interested." If a producer says, "Love the script, babe. Do you want to stop over at my house tonight to discuss it?" chances are, it's not the script he's interested in.

If someone in Hollywood tells you "the check is in the mail," don't start paying your bills, expecting to get the check within the week. I had a client who took that promise seriously, not understanding the subtext. He paid all his bills, sent them out in the mail, and continued to wait for the check, which he thought would come any day to cover his debts. Out of angst over the checks that would surely bounce within a week, he decided to rob a bank and ask for exactly the amount of money he needed to pay his bills — no more, no less. The bank was on the second floor of a building, which gave the manager and police enough time to prevent his exit. He was quickly arrested and served a year in prison.

No one ever explained the subtext to him, but it would have helped if he had understood it.

On the other hand, he went on to get several writing assignments and even got a movie made — which was what he wanted in the first place.

Cultural subtext can be confusing, because we don't know what something means, and often don't know enough about the culture to know whether the subtext even exists. We see how this clash of cultures can lead to misinterpretation and confusion in such films as *Dances with Wolves* (1990), *Witness* (1985), and *Whale Rider* (2002). Sometimes people living in a culture don't even recognize their own subtext and don't understand your inappropriate actions. Sometimes there is subtext, and sometimes there isn't.

Norms relate not only to international cultures and the film culture, but also to socioeconomics and class cultures. For instance, someone might not be aware that it is inappropriate to curl up in a chair or lie down on a sofa in a corporate lounge, or to wear tattered jeans or short skirts to most job interviews. The reactions, and the fact you didn't get the job, might give you a clue.

An attorney recounted the story of a young woman who came to a job interview in a very short skirt. They sat at a glass table and he found it was difficult to concentrate on her qualifications, considering the circumstances. He realized that someone who didn't understand appropriate attire for a job interview may not understand other aspects of corporate culture. Perhaps she was turned down for the job for other reasons as well, but this reason certainly came into play. She may not know why she didn't get the job, and it may be that the attorney would not find it appropriate to discuss this detail, but the result was the same — she didn't get the subtext and didn't get the job!

TRUSTING YOUR INTERPRETATION OF SUBTEXT

You might feel butterflies but don't know why you're nervous in a particular situation, or around a particular person. You might feel distrust. Sometimes we're told "everything is fine," but our gut tells us it isn't. And we often don't know whether to believe our gut or not.

We might feel this twinge in the presence of something really rotten, perhaps even some kind of evil, even though the person we meet seems perfectly fine. But something alerts us. Usually we simply feel that something is wrong.

In *The Fugitive* (1993), when Sam Gerard leaves the apartment of the One-Armed Man, he turns to his deputy and says, "This guy's dirty." Nothing was said in the text indicating that assessment, but Gerard senses that the guy isn't straight — and he is right.

I've experienced this feeling twice. I'm usually not a good judge of people because I figure everyone is "really nice" and "just fine." I have been wrong a number of times. But twice I met a person who made me feel there was something really wrong even though I could find no evidence for my feelings. In both cases, I had a brief interaction with the person and was more of an observer than a participant in the encounter. The first case was a very quick introduction to someone my colleague was talking to, someone whom she obviously had known for some time. I didn't understand why I had this feeling, or how I could get this feeling from a simple introduction. I watched the person conversing with my colleague and everything looked just fine. Later, I was told the person was very untrustworthy and manipulative — even described as a "bad person." I don't think my colleague knew it at the time, but discovered soon after. But I felt it and, trusting my feelings and instincts, sensed the truth behind the person's mask.

Another time I met a minister and had the same feeling, which again made little sense to me. I did notice that he didn't make eye contact and seemed distracted, but he was organizing an event, so I figured that was the reason. I still couldn't understand why I had this strange and uneasy feeling. Later, I learned he was having an affair with someone in his congregation and he was fired soon after that.

We have probably all had these intuitions about people and situations — times we have felt uneasy or have picked up on something subtle. We may have had a thought flit through our head, or a flash of insight, or a subtle feeling that alerted us.

Some people experience this sensation as a warning. Or, hey, this person seems to want something from you, but he's not saying it. Or, this person seems too attentive. It could come from an emotion, such as fear or discomfort, or from an intuition you don't understand. You might wonder why you had that thought, or shrug it off, but something is probably going on that is not being clearly seen or understood. Just as you can learn to trust your intuition in real life, you can learn to trust your interpretation of a character's behavior in film.

LOOK TO THE PAUSES FOR SUBTEXT

Sometimes subtext is communicated in the pauses. We have probably all had the experience of asking for directions. I've always figured that the longer the pause before you get an answer, the farther you will end up from where you want to go. "Do you know where St. James Plaza is?" Count: one, two, three seconds as you wait, and you know you're really far, or the person giving directions isn't sure. Well, that's the way it works in dialogue. You ask someone something — "Are you angry at your mother?" and if the pause is a long one, that's subtextually telling you something wrong here. Finally the answer comes, "Oh no, not in the least bit." But the pause told it all.

NOTICE THE SWERVES IN CONVERSATION

You can express subtext through swerves in the conversation. It may be that a character asks a direct question but does not get a direct answer. If we ask someone, "Why are you late?" and the person replies, "Have you any idea how hard it's raining out there?" we might notice the question was not answered.

If someone changes the conversation topic, we might figure there's subtext somewhere. Maybe someone unexpectedly enters the room and the two people talking suddenly start talking about something else. Sometimes characters speak at cross-purposes. In *Ordinary People* (1980, by Alvin Sargent from the novel by Judith Guest), the conversation between Beth and Conrad shows how very disconnected they are. Conrad unwittingly surprises Beth, who is sitting in Buck's bedroom.

BETH
I didn't think you were here.

CONRAD
... I just got in. I didn't know you were here.

BETH
I didn't play golf, today. It was cold.

CONRAD
How's your golf game?

BETH
I didn't play.

CONRAD
Oh... It did get colder today.

BETH
No, I mean... for the year it got colder.

CONRAD
Yeah.

Given all the possible interpretations, we might think the writer lets the audience figure out the subtext. But the point is not to confuse or merely to suggest, but rather to direct the audience to the interpretation that eventually leads to a fairly clear understanding of what's going on. The pieces may not all form the interpretation immediately. It might take the entire film, helped by the actor, director, and everyone else in the production before all the pieces fit together to form a cohesive, unified film. This work takes a careful selection of words, scenes, and characters. The writer must try to avoid detours and misinterpretations that result in arbitrary scenes and dialogue.

Many writers write the text in the first draft and then start shading in the subtext in future drafts. They keep moving away from on-the-nose dialogue to layer the script.

Perhaps you start working on a scene by thinking about what you want to get across. Maybe the man has to communicate he's attracted to the woman. In the first draft, he might say, "I'm attracted to you," or "You interest me!" But as you continue to work with the scene (remembering it might take five or ten or more rewrites), you might put the text on one side of the page and the subtext on the other side of the page. Or, you might write the subtext underneath or above the lines, as I've done with the scenes above.

You might brainstorm what subtext you want to get across. Is the man desperate, and looking for a girlfriend or wife. Is he looking everyone over? Is he totally smitten, but realizes he's not good enough for her, perhaps because of his class, or financial situation, or race? Or maybe it's a woman attracted to a woman or a man attracted to a man, who has to find out, through subtext, innuendo, and suggestion, whether the other person is gay or not. Whatever technique is used by the writer, the job includes shading in subtext. Drama and life are more than just good text.

WHERE ELSE DO WE FIND SUBTEXT?

Although it is usually thought of as *beneath* the words, subtext can be expressed in other ways. In film especially, subtext can become clear to the audience through words, gestures, attitudes, actions, and reactions. The writer creates the gestures, actions, and emotions of the character, which get further expressed by the director and actor. The writer creates images that will be further expressed by the art director and cinematographer. The writer's ability to use the language of cinema to express hidden layers often marks the difference between a great writer and the merely competent. If the subtext is well-crafted, the audience understands these hidden layers — and stories, themes, and characters — become richer as a result. When the writer does subtext the script is terrific and the film is great.

EXERCISES AND QUESTIONS FOR DISCUSSION

(1) Make a list of times in your life when you have encountered subtext in conversations with others. What did the person say? What did the person mean? How did you respond to the feeling that you weren't hearing the total truth? How long did it take you to figure out the subtext?

(2) Have you encountered subtext in other cultures, whether through cultures of a different ethnic, national, or social background, or a different class or economic background? How did you figure out the subtext? Did someone ever discuss it with you?

(3) Has your intuition ever told you that something going on was "bad" or "evil," but your logic wanted to deny this feeling? Did you feel there was subtext in the situation? Did you later find out you were correct?

(4) Look at a film that deals with hidden psychological problems, such as *The Soloist* (2009), *The Three Faces of Eve* (1957), or *Sybil* (1976). How does the film convey the problems that are beneath the surface?

(5) Do you have favorite examples of subtext from films that either amuse you, or that you find especially powerful?

expressing subtext through words: character information and backstory

Words imply. Words suggest. Words point to meaning. Some words work better than others. To reveal the subtext, words aren't arbitrary, but are often written and rewritten and re-written some more to make sure the subtext comes through in spite of the text. Great writers know their job — to find the right word, the best word, and to let the subtext shine beneath the words.

How do you find the right word? How do you figure out what subtext is, and where do you put it? You can begin by thinking about the various elements that make up character and construct a character biography that suggests possibilities for subtext.

WHAT'S THE CHARACTER'S BIO?

There are two views on writing, or thinking about, a character bio. Some writers find it very helpful to list information about their character, much as you would if you were writing a resume or a biography of yourself for a job. They think about all aspects of the character's backstory and of the present and past life —

who they are, what they like, what kind of parents they have, how many children are in the family, what grades they got in school, and so forth.

Other writers don't find this exercise helpful. In much the same way that a resume can be dry and overly factual without giving a feeling for the personality of the person, this exercise, according to some writers, doesn't do much to bring the character alive. However, even these writers often find thinking through a part of the character's background is helpful, especially if it relates directly to some aspect of the story.

If you're going to create subtext, you need to know some facts about your character. Whether you create these facts consciously, or whether you intuit them, they still need to inform your writing in order to create a great character.

Characters talk and act in the present, implying a background filled with experiences — both negative and positive — about their childhood and adulthood. In most cases, the audience doesn't need to know all about the characters' education or what they did when they were three or seven, how many siblings they have and all about the house where they grew up, who they played with and how they did in school. Some of this information may be important, or at least can add layers to the character, but sometimes writers put far too much of this information into the text when it only belongs in the subtext.

The subtext can often be found in what the character doesn't put on his or her resume. Most job applicants aren't willing to tell the employer they were fired a number of times, or went bankrupt, or were once arrested for embezzlement. They don't want the employer to know about their unhappy childhood and that they are currently in therapy, or on medication, which might affect their job. They want to conceal that they're habitually late, and tend to over-eat when nervous. They don't want to let others know they tend to take reams of paper home from the office supply closet (along with a stapler and some printer cartridges), and that they have three cats, two more than their apartment allows. (Two are put in the closet when the landlady comes).

The character is applying for a job in your script. His job description will include the bad and the good, the flaws and the talents, the insecurities and where he feels competent and confident. Therefore, the character has to convey information to the writer, and to the audience, to prove he is a good applicant for the job. Some of the information about your character that comes from your creative unconscious may surprise you, just as you might be surprised about what you mention and what you remember as you make out your own resume.

WHERE ELSE DO WE FIND SUBTEXT?

In creating this biography, add another piece of information that you would rarely put on a resume — the character's attitude about the information. With attitude, emotions, conflicts, personality, and even dynamic relationships with other characters begin to take shape. Attitude suggests subtext, and will begin to create the rich underpinnings of the character. For every fact, you might also think of the character's response to this information.

The Character's Age: Most resumes used to begin by stating age. Although requesting this fact is illegal now, most of your scripts will have some mention of the character's age, especially for major characters. Unfortunately, many writers use the same cliché for their main characters: She's described as "late 20s or early 30s, pretty and sexy." He's usually described as "mid to late 30s, ruggedly handsome." Many times writers simply say "attractive," which tells us very little except what almost every major character will be, with only a few exceptions. Sometimes, by the time a producer reads it for the 300th time, this

38

descriptor becomes tiresome and not very imaginative. And, it doesn't make an actor want to play the role. There's nothing actable in this description; it only depends on whether the actors look their age or not, and whether there's good make-up, lighting, and a costume person who can make them as attractive as possible.

But the approximate age is important, after all, the producer and director have to figure out who to cast.

You begin inserting subtext into the description and dialogue by thinking about how your characters feel about their age. In *Fatal Attraction* (1987, by James Deardon) the description at the beginning of the script tells us a world of information about Alex, and sets up the motivation for the desperate actions that follow. Although the audience won't see the description, the producer, actor, director, costumer, and make-up person will see it — and it will inform the physical presentation of the character.

Deardon writes: "She must be in her thirties, but she dresses younger, trendily, and gets away with it."

What does this tell us about Alex? She's not happy about her age. She wants to be younger. As the story evolves, Alex is clearly getting desperate — she wants to fall in love, have a child, and probably wants to get married. She is driven by this desperation, although she's much too professional to show it. In her initial meeting with Dan, and probably with men in general, she tries to portray herself as a "with it" professional — attractive, willing, wild, fun, and exciting. But it only takes one night with Alex for Dan, and the audience, to realize how dangerous she is. With just this much information, Glenn Close could have begun to think through the dimensions and layers she would bring to the role. She was nominated for an Academy Award for her stunning performance of a very well-developed character.

SKILLS, TALENTS, AND ABILITIES

Most of the time, when a character possesses special abilities, we see it in the text and it plays out in the story. If someone is a boxer, or practices martial arts, or plays the piano, or is a skilled mountain climber, this quality will be shown in the film and pay off later in the story as we see the skill leading the character to compete in a music contest or fight in a championship match.

Their skills might also pay off later in the way they approach a problem. A pianist might tinker on the piano while trying to find a way to let his girlfriend know he doesn't want to see her anymore. A mountain climber might be the first person to run to help someone in physical danger, whether it's on a mountain or not. These innate strengths and learned skills can be used to show how the character approaches any number of situations. All of these skills and reactions might be in the text.

There still might be subtext in the attitudes the person has toward these abilities. It might be that the person seems overly confident and talks big, but underneath he is unsure about any chance of competing and this anxiety shows in the very way he tries to hide his nervousness. Or, maybe the person is very talented, but is afraid people won't like her if she wins, so she sabotages her performance and makes dozens of mistakes. Sometimes people lie about their abilities, either to get out of responsibility, or because they lack confidence.

Sometimes subtext comes through in films about people with special psychic abilities. At times, they try to deny their gift, until it pushes at them and they have no choice but to listen and accept it. In the television series *Medium*, the main character, Allison DuBois, has visions and dreams of dead people. But having this gift isn't always easy, and in the series, she has to learn to come to grips with and even control her abilities. As a result, she uses her power to solve crimes.

In the *Spiderman* series, Peter Parker has to come to terms with his abilities. In *Spiderman 2*, he has an identity crisis and comes to the conclusion that he doesn't want to be Spiderman. He throws away his suit and chooses to be normal. This choice is in the text. It's a clear action and by the time it occurs, we understand it. But we understand it because the subtext rumblings have prepared us. We know he's torn between being Spiderman and his love for Mary Jane. We see him at times take off his mask as if he's considering taking off the entire costume. There are other subtextual resonances before he throws out his suit. Mary Jane is in the play *The Importance of Being Earnest* (1910, by Oscar Wilde). The first time she appears, he misses the performance — which suggests that he is missing the importance of being honest and "being earnest." But he goes to the second performance, after he's decided to be normal. He later decides to accept that "with great power comes great responsibility," reclaiming his suit and his identity.

A similar story is found in *Superman 2*, when Superman wants to be normal because of his love for Lois Lane. He gives up his powers, only to take them back when he realizes the world is in grave danger. In *Superman 2*, more of this information is in the text than in the subtext.

The Character's Educational Background: If a person's educational background is important, that information will usually be in the text. The M.D. will be addressed as "Dr. Smith," or Indiana Jones, with his PhD, will be addressed as "Dr. Jones." Another person's education might be addressed because he mentions his alma mater ("I'm a Harvard man"), or she mentions where she studied, "I studied at the High School of Performing Arts in New York — I act!" or because he might simply be performing the actions that show his education — walking down the hospital hall wearing a nurse's uniform; filling prescriptions behind the pharmacy counter; teaching in a high school or college; or wearing a badge, which tells us he is

a detective with the NYPD. There's no subtext with this basic 41
information. It simply tells us through visuals, or with a line or
two, something about the person's educational level.

But subtext comes with attitude. What does the person think
about his or her education? How does the person feel about his
or her educational level? Some who have had little schooling
might be ashamed or they might be proud. They might say, "I
don't have no book learnin', but look what I made of myself!
I'm really somethin'!"

Or, they might not be willing to admit their lack of education,
but it shows in their vocabulary and grammar and attitudes and
sometimes through their lack of knowledge of basics that most
people learn in high school or college. If the neighbor guy
says to you, "Who's Shakespeare? He that guy moved in next
door?" we immediately know a whole range of information.
If a teacher tells this neighbor about William Shakespeare, she
might be showing her attitude about a lack of learning or her
enthusiasm for Shakespeare.

Subtext might come into the conversation if we wonder why the
teacher is talking about Shakespeare with the neighbor anyway.
Is this conversation meant to embarrass the neighbor? Or, to
show how erudite — and therefore better — the teacher is? Or, is
the neighbor fascinated with new information, and welcomes it?

I know some PhDs who are a bit embarrassed by their degree
and don't tell anyone about it, and others who insist everyone
use it, even close friends. There are some people who don't
like to call someone "doctor," perhaps out of a lack of respect
for education, and others who use it all the time. I once knew
a woman from my home town who was the wife of a doctor.
When referring to her husband, she never called him by his
first name, but always by the title of "Dr." Of course, for some
women, marrying a doctor was a big coup. This reference told
me volumes about how she sensed her role as a wife and her

pride in being married to the only doctor in town. (It was a small town!)

I had a short-lived relationship with a guy who was so proud of my doctorate, he made sure I met his parents on our first (and only) date so he could introduce me as "Dr. Seger." Too much subtext going on there!

Educational level can be suggested in other ways. We know a character did well in school or at least is very smart when she uses vocabulary or grammar that suggests a high degree of education. We know the character has read a fair amount of Shakespeare if he refers to someone by saying she's "just like the dark lady of the Sonnets" — although he might leave the audience behind with that remark.

Sometimes a character's attitude toward education can be expressed through the words on the T-shirt he or she is wearing. Are they crass? ("Screw you, bud!"); or purposefully un-educated? ("I ain't got no education — on purpose!"); or purposefully obscure ("I'm Jude the Obscure — deal with it!"); or, perhaps implying their subject matter — mathematical formulas, musical notes, or a line from Tennessee Williams.

Characters have often had bad experiences with school. Perhaps they say: "Just like school! Not my idea of fun!" or "Don't send me back to that prison!"

Conflict can come about by the contrast between the parents' attitude toward education and the children's attitude. The first child in a family to go to college may be treated better (or worse) by the parents. The child who became a doctor might be treated like a king, while the other siblings and the working class relatives are ignored.

HOW MUCH MONEY DO THEY HAVE?

The educational level may relate to the economic class of the character. Although statistically those with education make more money than those without, plenty of stories exist in which the person with very little education becomes a millionaire. The amount of money may be in the text, but the character's attitude toward the money may be in the subtext.

There are stories of children who grew up believing they were poor, only to discover their family had a great deal of money stashed away, but were ashamed of it or afraid of losing it all so they kept it a secret or gave it away or squandered it.

I had the opposite experience. I grew up believing we had enough – not rich, but definitely not poor. When I was in my 40s, my mother told me that we had been poor when I was growing up, but she didn't want us to know because she didn't want us to get a complex about it. She had grown up in a family that always talked about being poor and always talked about money, so she decided she wouldn't raise her children that way. I was amazed, even shocked by this information; it shifted my perspective of my childhood. At first, I couldn't understand how it could be true because I didn't remember ever feeling poor, nor did I ever perceive our family as poor. I grew up with a beautiful Steinway Concert Grand Piano in our living room (my mother was a piano teacher), and I knew poor people didn't have pianos – certainly not ones like that. My mother retold a long story of how we happened to get that piano, clarifying that it didn't prove we were rich. She reminded me of the Thanksgiving when we ate hot dogs instead of turkey. My sister and I thought that was great. She explained that she served hot dogs because there was nothing else in the refrigerator and she and my dad had no money left. Everything had been represented to us so we didn't think we were poor. At times there was more money, so being poor was not the case for all of my childhood, but her revelation showed me how something can be interpreted one way, but not be the whole story.

By the time most people reach adulthood, they have some religious background and some attitudes about religion. They might have grown up attending a church, synagogue, mosque, ashram, or some spiritual community — or not. They might have left it, or become more committed and involved as they got older. If they left, they might have left amiably, or they might still carry the resentment of what happened to them in synagogue or how they responded when the kid in Sunday school said they were going to hell, or how they became increasingly uncomfortable as their spiritual community radicalized.

In many cases, you won't need to mention this aspect. But these religious attitudes also inform a person's attitude toward others, and show up in the ways they speak and behave. They might make snide remarks about religious people, or about people of specific religions. Someone who's uncomfortable being alone might be highly uncomfortable around the mystic who meditates three hours a day. Someone might become religiously and socially radicalized and start attending peace protests, or perhaps a Tea Party protest, or a pro-choice or pro-life march. This behavior might make a parent, spouse, or friend wonder what has caused that nice, socially appropriate person to suddenly respond in this way.

Attitude, or information about someone's religious context, can come out in a small piece of dialogue here or there, if it's appropriate.

In *Raider's of the Lost Ark* (1981), two lines tell us a great deal about Indiana Jones and his attitude toward religion.

Indiana tells the government agents about the city of Tanis and about the Lost Ark that is supposed to lie there. When he sees their bewildered faces, he says:

                    INDIANA JONES
        Didn't you guys ever go to Sunday school?

Right away, we know Jones has a Protestant background since Catholics go to Catechism, devout Jews study the Torah and go to shul, and Protestants go to Sunday School.

This information may not seem relevant, except the whole film is based on the Bible's story of the Lost Ark and the few references to Tanis made in the Bible. Although from this reference, we don't know what Jones believes now, later he implies he's an agnostic or atheist. When Jones shows the government men a picture of what the Ark might look like, one of the government men asks him about the light coming out of the Ark and Jones replies:

<pre>
                    INDIANA JONES
... the power of God... if you believe in that sort of thing.
</pre>

In that line, Jones implies his attitude and his current belief system. He also reveals a cynicism that sets up where he stands at the beginning of the film, and which transforms as the film proceeds.

In *The Great Santini*, Toomer, the young black man who stutters, tells us a world about what his life is like with a simple line. Ben and Toomer are watching the stars and Ben points out a shooting star. Ben mentions it's a shooting star, but Toomer has a more religious interpretation:

<pre>
                     TOOMER
      That's the tear of infant Jesus falling on
      account of such a sinful and hateful world.
</pre>

Toomer has plenty to deal with. Although he's a man of faith, he knows the oppression and the nastiness that's out there.

SUBTEXT SUGGESTS OUR TRUE DESIRES, WANTS, AND GOALS

Often we're afraid to talk about what truly interests us, or what our true desires are. This reluctance might be because others won't agree with us or may think the subject is not appropriate for polite company, or because we'll never achieve the object of our desires — according to parents or close friends. So we hide what we truly want and say what we think others want to hear. In *Dead Poets Society* (1989), Neil really wants to write and act, but his father makes it clear he's not to do extracurricular activities. He's to focus on grades. When the other boys start to sympathize with him, Neil replies, "I don't care." But clearly he does.

In the A & E Production of *Pride and Prejudice*, (1996, by Seth Grahame-Smith from the book by Jane Austen), Charlotte has recently married Mr. Collins, the rector, a man who had been interested in Lizzie but she decidedly was not interested in him. He is a bit of a silly man, full of himself, clearly more than a bit of a bore with his bragging and name-dropping, while pretending to be a man of importance. Charlotte understands her husband. She is also clear about what she really wanted all along — a husband, a home in the country, and stability. Although Lizzie might need to marry for love (which is implied throughout the film, as well as in this scene), Charlotte doesn't have the same need.

When Lizzie visits Charlotte after her marriage, Charlotte looks out the window at her husband and begins the scene:

CHARLOTTE
Mr. Collins tends the gardens himself and spends
a good part of every day in them.

Already, we might be picking up on subtext. If he's spending a good part of every day in his garden, he is probably not spending a good part of the day with Charlotte. We might wonder, "How does Charlotte feel about that?"

LIZZIE
The exercise must be very beneficial.

If you watch the film, Lizzie seems to be already picking up on the subtext from Charlotte. Her response is deliberately

neutral in order to elicit more from Charlotte — if Charlotte
so chooses to tell her more.

>   CHARLOTTE
>   Oh yes. I encourage him to be in his gardens as much as
>   possible. And then he has to walk to Rosings
>   nearly every day.

Oh! So, Charlotte encourages him. Now we understand that
her husband spends a great deal of time in the garden and takes
long walks to town. We're beginning to get the picture here.

>   LIZZIE
>   So often. Is that necessary?

Hmmm, what is going on in this marriage?

>   CHARLOTTE
>   Perhaps not, but I confess I encourage that as well.

Oh, Charlotte encourages all of this. We're beginning to get the
picture here.

>   LIZZIE
>   Walking is very beneficial exercise.

Lizzie likes to walk, and she might wonder if all this exercise is
all about a love for walking, although Lizzie is not known to be
dense and already seems to understand what's going on. Again,
she remains fairly neutral. It wouldn't be polite to ask Charlotte
outright if she likes to be alone, loves the little house, and recognizes that her husband is not good company.

>   CHARLOTTE
>   Indeed it is. And when he is in the house, he's mostly in
>   his bookroom which affords a good view of the
>   road whenever Lady Catherine's carriage should
>   drive by.

Oh, he's in his own place, and... where is she?

                    LIZZIE
        And you prefer to sit in this parlor?

                   CHARLOTTE
    Yes, so it often happens that a whole day passes in
      which we have not spent more than a few moments
                in each other's company.

And it's so blissful on those days! Very nice, indeed.

                    LIZZIE
                    I see.

Yes, Lizzie now sees the subtext very clearly. So do we!

                   CHARLOTTE
    I find that I can bear the solitude very cheerfully.
    Often I find myself quite content with my situation.

And now she tells us, fairly specifically, this setup is just how she wants it. But she's still putting a bit of subtext in the scene by using the word "bear." It's not perfect, but she can usually be content.

If you watch the scene, you'll notice how the characters use glances at each other and at Mr. Collins outside the window to communicate subtext. In this case, Charlotte is conscious of the subtext and willing to share it with Lizzie, but it wouldn't be appropriate for the characters during that historical period to state outright all of these meanings. Nor would it be such a brilliant scene if it were just about the text.

EXPRESSING SUBTEXT THROUGH THE SHADOW

If we're really honest with ourselves, we probably admit we have some kind of psychological problem — uncertainties, insecurities, a few irrational fears here or there, something we're obsessed with, a bit too negative about some things. Like us, characters do not have it all together, and their flaws drive them and give them dimension.

Sometimes the psychology in a character or a family is expressed   49
emotionally. Their feelings of disappointment or discourage-
ment, regret or anger at how things are drive them to emotional
outbursts, where suddenly they react way out of proportion to
what is going on.

Almost all the characters in the film *American Beauty* (1999, by
Alan Ball) are driven by emotional subtext. Lester is going
through a midlife crisis and suddenly realizes things could be
different. He quits his job, blackmails his boss, and puts down
new rules in the household − including changing the dinner
music. His wife, Carolyn, holds to her upper middle class life-
style. She has her own set of secrets − she's having an affair. The
neighbors have secrets. The mother is abused by the husband,
and takes it silently, not expressing herself. The military father
is a closet homosexual.

These psychological problems, flaws, and imperfections often
exist in what psychologists call "the shadow," that part of us we
want to deny, which is the opposite of what we portray to the
world. The idea of the shadow can be seen very clearly in the
classic *Dr. Jekyll and Mr. Hyde*, from the novel by Robert Louis
Stevenson. The story shows the two sides of a character − the
good and the evil. The kindly Dr. Jekyll experiments with his
shadow side, transforming himself through a potion into the
evil Mr. Hyde.

The book and film *The Picture of Dorian Gray* (1945) puts the
shadow side of Dorian into a painting that changes as Dorian
becomes more dissolute and evil. He, however, remains youthful and sweet-looking, in spite of the evil in his soul.

We can see the shadow pop out in such films as *L.A. Confidential*
(1997) and *Witness*, when the chief of police who seems to be
pursuing the bad guy is really one of them.

For the seemingly confident sports figure, the shadow might be the looming insecurities that threaten the upcoming competition.

For the political figure who tries to project family values, it's the affair he's having on the sly (we've seen more than a few of those!)

For the seemingly honest corporate man, it's the dishonesty he tries to hide — stealing from the supply cabinet, fudging overtime hours, cheating on taxes.

For the law-and-order cop who says he abides by all the rules, it's the corruption on the side.

Most characters try to keep their shadows hidden, but they emerge at some time or another. We are usually surprised because the shadow starkly contrasts to the side of us, or the side of another, that we usually see.

There are characters with hidden secrets that fall within the scope of psychologically normal, and then there are, of course, other characters who are just plain wacko, but won't admit it. The shadow keeps popping out in words and actions, revealing the true character beneath.

In *Psycho* (1960, written by Joseph Stefano), Norman Bates is truly psycho. He clearly has a whole slew of unresolved feelings about his mother. He explains to Mary Crane.

NORMAN
When you love someone, you don't do
that to them even if you hate them.
Oh, I don't hate her. I hate...
what she's become. I hate the illness.

Hate? Love? How does Norman really feel? Both — in spite of denying his true feelings.

Although the shadow is usually thought of as the negative side, it can be any contrast to the side we show to the world — negative or positive. It is simply the unexpressed, buried, unknown, and hidden side of us. In film the shadow is usually negative because having it so provides more opportunity for conflict, emotion, and flaws in the character. But it can also be positive. Under certain circumstances, an insecure person might suddenly find a new level of confidence. The dishonest person might be honest about certain things and surprise us (and maybe even herself).

In *Up in the Air*, Ryan seems content to be solitary, traveling all the time, uncommitted; but his shadow wants to be connected. He's greatly disappointed to find out that his mistress has a family. His disappointment seems to come not just from her betrayal, but also from his interest in her, which seems to be far more than just a one or two-night stand. Elsewhere, he makes the commitment to go to his niece's wedding, talks to her fiancé when he gets cold feet, and even volunteers to walk her down the aisle — showing he wants to take a more active part in his family. His shadow is quite different than the persona of one who wants to sustain very few commitments.

In *Up* (2009) the protagonist is bitter and living in the past. A young kid in need of a father accidentally comes along. The companionship forces the man's growth and acceptance of his shadow side. We can see that the shadow was positive — he was a loving husband — a side of himself he has covered up since his wife died. We can see the bitterness underneath, which comes from his tremendous sense of loss and disappointment for having let his wife down by not pursuing their dreams of adventure. As the story proceeds, we see he has a genuine desire to feel love. By the end, he reconciles with his shadow side and is willing to express his kinder self.

SUBTEXT SHOWS DENIAL, ATTITUDES, AND COVER-UPS:

Sometimes people are dismissive or evasive because they don't want to confront what's really going on. They try to get out of facing issues, or being honest when it doesn't benefit them.

In *Revolutionary Road* (2008, by Justin Haythe), after Jack Wheeler has gotten the secretary quite drunk and slept with her, he gets dressed, ready to go back to his wife. Clearly the secretary is waiting for some words of encouragement, compliments, or commitment. Instead, he tells her "Listen, you were swell" and kisses her on the cheek. We might think: "What was that all about? 'Swell!?' You've got to be kidding!" It's not exactly what a woman wants to hear. Yet, we know what it's all about. Jack does not want to make any commitment to her, but wants to be nice about it. He wants to leave the fling open-ended, but doesn't want to give her any reason to think it's more than a little afternoon delight before going home to his conventional 1950s home.

When Jack and April announce they're moving to Paris, neighbors and friends see the idea as rather juvenile, an attitude that is implied through words suggestive of immaturity. Millie, the next-door neighbor, says, "Sounds wonderful, kids!" but the word "kids" implies her opinion of this idea. Throughout the film, the plan is called "immature," "whimsical," "fantasy," "a childish idea," and "unrealistic." When Frank cancels the trip, and April becomes increasingly frenetic and frantic about her dreams dying, even Frank implies the childishness of the dream and suggests that she see a "shrink." He doesn't use the word "psychologist," "therapist," or "psychiatrist," or say "you have to get help," but uses the word, "shrink." "Shrink" has many associations. It's a negative word, usually implying that the person needing to see a shrink is a bit crazy. "Shrink" also suggests what is going on — April's dreams must be "shrunk" (to the point of disappearing), and the shrink is supposed to serve that effort by helping her see that her dreams are too big, too unrealistic, too extravagant, too grandiose.

Whereas "shrink" denotes making something smaller, the word "army," as used by Uncle Charlie in *Shadow of Doubt* (1943), denotes a larger force. He tells his sister, Emma:

```
                UNCLE CHARLIE                          53
       Children should be brought up to know what
       the world is really like. They should be
            prepared... like an army...
```

And through his word choice, we might think: "Obviously, Charlie thinks of the world as the enemy, an enemy that must be defeated."

The writer carefully chooses the right word to add depth and resonance to the character and to the story. "Army" implies conquering, aggression, defeating, getting the upper hand, or overcoming. "Army" has a violent resonance, just like "murder." Armies also kill, just like Uncle Charlie.

A world of information about the character can be revealed through words that imply and suggest backstory and attitude. Every word is carefully chosen. No word is vague. No word is arbitrary.

54   EXERCISES AND QUESTIONS FOR DISCUSSION

(1) Think of films you love. What do you know about the character's backstory? How do you know it? How much is in the text? How much in the subtext?

(2) Can you think of films with religious characters? How are their religious attitudes implied? What do you know about their religion just from a character saying "I'm Catholic," or "I'm Baptist," or "I'm Muslim"? Does the character have an attitude toward his or her religious beliefs and actions?

(3) Watch a film of your choosing and write out the resume of the character based upon what you have learned about the character in the film. How much of this information did you get from the text? How much from the subtext?

(4) Make a list or google to get information about films that show people with special abilities or disabilities, whether physical or psychic or mental. Watch several. Contrast the different attitudes characters have toward their abilities. Then, think about the psychology in your own script. If you're working with a mental disease, does the character try to hide it? If so, how is this hiding done? Through denial? By keeping a tight lid on talk and emotions?

You might decide to talk to a psychiatrist or read books on the subject and ask how the disease manifests, how the person usually tries to hide it, and how it reveals itself.

(5) Do any of your characters have a secret, something they keep hidden? Is it something they feel guilty about? Ashamed of? Is it illegal? Immoral? Inappropriate? If so, how does it pop out — when the character is alone, or with others?

CHAPTER THREE

techniques for expressing subtext through words

Choosing the right word, the word with many associations, is the usual way to suggest subtext, but other techniques can be helpful when trying to convey what lies beneath.

USING SIMILES TO EXPRESS SUBTEXT

Whenever a character says one thing is "like" another, the simile brings to mind layers of associations. If a character says, "Our love is like a rose in bloom," our minds immediately drift to associations with the freshness of a rose, like the freshness of new-found love, the beginning of love like the beginning of spring, the youth of love, like a dewy rose. The use of the word "like" moves beyond simply saying, "We are newly in love!" "Like" forces other associations to come to mind, so we can see below the surface.

In *The Godfather: Part II* (1974, by Mario Puzo and Frances Ford Coppola), Kay announces to her husband, Michael, that she didn't have a miscarriage, she had an abortion, adding, "Just like our marriage is an abortion." The associations that come to mind may be many — how the life of their marriage has been

56

destroyed, removed, cut off, or put to an end by Michael's criminal activities; how Kay may have been calling the problem in their marriage a "miscarriage" when it was far more than that. Perhaps there are associations with killing, murder, and destruction — much like Michael's life has been about killing, murder, and destruction, and how that affects their marriage. The more associations that fit the metaphor, the richer the dialogue can be.

Sometimes a simile is implied, rather than expressed. Rather than using the word "like," the dialogue suggests one thing is like another but takes out the word "like." This is the difference between a simile and a metaphor. In *Blindside* (2009), Leigh Anne (Sandra Bullock) is described by her husband in the following way: "She's an onion. You have to peel her back a layer at a time." The film *To Have and Have Not* (1944) moves even further away from the simile, while still implying one thing is like another. In the film, Slim (Lauren Bacall) says to the wife of the wounded resistance fighter as she serves her breakfast, "The eggs may be a little hard-boiled." The wife answers, "I like them that way!" The wife has just had an encounter with Steve (Humphrey Bogart) and has decided she can trust him. She likes her eggs hard-boiled, just like she likes men hard-boiled and tough enough to handle the situation.

IMPLYING, THEN SAYING THE SUBTEXT

Occasionally subtext is suggested, then said outright. This sequence usually takes place when one character shows confusion over the meaning of a line. In *As Good as it Gets* (1997, story by Mark Andrus, screenplay by Mark Andrus and James L. Brooks) — in one of my favorite lines in any film — Melvin pays Carol a compliment over dinner. He starts by telling her he has a disorder and that a pill can sometimes help it. He says he hates pills, really hates them. He then pays her a compliment, explaining that after seeing her one night, "I started taking my pills." Many of us may have gotten the subtext with this line — if

he started taking pills he hates, he must like her and be willing
to do what is necessary to become the kind of man she would
like. But just in case we didn't get it, he follows with a second
line, which puts the subtext into the text.

```
                       MELVIN
          You make me want to be a better man.
```

It's not unusual to have a character imply subtext, and have
another character say, "What do you mean?" to which the character responds. This method can be too on-the-nose, but with
some variation, (as in the example above), it helps convey an
important point.

STOPPING THE SENTENCE TO IMPLY SUBTEXT

Sometimes a character almost says the subtext, but then stops in
the middle of a word, or in the middle of a sentence. In *As Good
as it Gets*, Carol and Melvin go to a fancy restaurant for dinner,
but the maitre'd tells Melvin he has to wear a coat and tie. He's
not happy about putting on some germ-infested coat supplied
by the restaurant so he goes out to buy a new outfit. When he
returns, Carol looks at him and starts to say:

```
                       CAROL
          You look so s---, you look great!
```

It seems she started to say, "You look so sexy," but stopped herself. After all, she's the one who said she would never sleep with
him, but she now finds he's quite attractive.

In *Psycho*, Norman shows Mary around the motel room, pointing
out the hangers, the soft mattress, and then starting to point
out the bathroom, but it's embarrassing to him to mention the
word; instead, he says, "and... the... over there... " as he points
to the bathroom and blushes. This awkwardness, of course, begins
to give us some insight into Norman's psychology. Here he just
seems a little strange, but we soon learn he's deranged.

58

In Psycho, Sam tells Mary, after another lunch-time sexual get-together in a shabby hotel room, that he'd like "a private island where we can run around without our... shoes on." He's wishing for an island where they can run around without their clothes on, but Mary has just asked for more respectability in their relationship, so he quickly changes his words. We still know what he means.

In *Shadow of a Doubt* (1943, by Thornton Wilder, Sally Benson, and Alma Reville, from a story by Gordon McDowell), Uncle Charlie talks about being tired of running. He starts a sentence:

>   CHARLIE
>   I was going to... well... then
>   I got the idea of coming out here.

We presume he was going to say, "I was going to kill myself." Notice, in each of these instances, how specific the sentence is in order to suggest the subtext without directly telling us. Words are carefully chosen to imply the true meaning. "You look sexy," "I was going to kill myself," and "Let's run around without our clothes on" are sentences we've probably heard before. When the sentence is completed with different words, we still get the meaning. We complete the sentence in our minds as it's meant to be said.

MISINTEPRETING THE SUBTEXT

Sometimes people misinterpret the subtext. They might think someone is attracted to them when the person is just being nice. They might think someone is in love with them, when they like each other and are really just good buddies, at least according to one person in the relationship. At some point, the events that follow, or perhaps a conversation, will correct the misinterpretation.

Years ago, a friend of mine thought the man she loved was in love with her. She detailed her interpretation for me, based on very subtle signs. In one case, she told me: "We both like the same china." She thought this shared taste meant they were suited for each other and that he loved her and was thinking of marriage. She was wrong. He simply liked the same china she did. She ended up marrying his roommate instead.

In *As Good as it Gets*, after Melvin helps Carol by paying for her son's medical tests and bills, Carol reaches the conclusion he's doing so in order to sleep with her. When she confronts him, telling him what she thinks is the subtext and clarifying that she will never sleep with him, he's confused and both are embarrassed by the mistaken interpretation. It seems she was wrong about his intentions. His actions showed how he was learning to care about someone else. It's possible to make the case that deep in his unconscious he really was sexually interested in her, because he kisses her at the end. But the prime motivation seems to be his developing care about her and his son.

In *The Messenger* (2009, by Alessandro Camon and Oren Moverman), Staff Sgt. Will Montgomery (Ben Foster) and Captain Tony Stone (Woody Harrelson) have a job to do: notify the next-of-kin (N.O.K.) when their husbands, wives, sons, or daughters have died in combat. In most cases, the N.O.K. are grief-stricken or enraged. But when they notify Olivia Pitterson, her reaction is muted and very strange. She thanks them, tells them their job must be difficult, gets the information from them, and then says goodbye. Her reaction is unusual, which Stone interprets for Montgomery, telling him what he thinks is the subtext.

```
                    STONE
          She's banging someone. See that shirt she
was hanging? Her husband dies 10,000 miles away. She's got a
            man on the clothesline already.
```

60

But Captain Stone was wrong about the subtext. Later, Olivia tells Will about her husband. He had re-enlisted to go back to Iraq several times, and he began to be a different man as a result of his experiences there.

> OLIVIA
> I missed him but I didn't miss the guy who had just left. I missed the man he was a long time ago...

Then she explains the real reason the shirt was on the clothesline.

> OLIVIA
> One morning, I opened the closet and his shirt fell out... It smelled awful... it smelled of rage and fear. It smelled of the man that he had become over there... anyway, I washed the shirt. And then you came.

In *Remains of the Day*, Miss Kenton believes there's a reason that Mr. Stevens did not want to hire Lizzie — because she's a very pretty girl, and Stevens seems uncomfortable having pretty girls on the staff. She then continues, clarifying the subtext as she understands it.

> MISS KENTON
> Might it be that our Mr. Stevens fears distraction? Can it be that our Mr. Stevens is flesh and blood after all and cannot trust himself?

She is on to something here, but it isn't about Lizzie. By the end of the film (in case we didn't get it earlier), we know Mr. Stevens was attracted to Miss Kenton and vice versa, but he didn't know what to do about it.

In *The Great Santini*, the mother, Lil, tells her son Ben what it means when his father is so harsh with him.

> LIL
> Because he loves you and he wants you to be the best.

But Ben doesn't buy it. He clarifies why she's wrong.   61

BEN
I love you. Punch.
I want you to be the best. Kick.

But Lil keeps interpreting. "That's the only way he knows how to say 'I'm sorry.'" Who is right? Lil has a point, but Ben knows enough to question love expressed through violence.

CHOOSING THE RIGHT WORD FOR RESONANCE

We understand subtext because the writer has carefully chosen the words with the most resonance. These words are not arbitrary. The writer didn't just put down the first word that came to mind. Nor is it a vague word or a cliché, unless the vague word (such as "nice" or "swell") actually resonates.

In *Remains of the Day*, Mr. Stevens has to find a new housekeeper because the former housekeeper and underbutler "ran off together last month." A number of words could have been used to let us know these two people were no longer working at Darlington's great home. He might have said, "They left together" or "eloped" or "quit." But "ran off" has a whole other series of implications. There's a sense of judgment here – Stevens obviously doesn't think highly of anything improper, especially two people who don't have the decency to stay and get married in an appropriate ceremony. It also tells us they left him in the lurch. They didn't quit and give two weeks notice. They took off.

The use of the phrase "run off" also implies how Stevens is trapped by convention.

Throughout the film, Stevens shows himself to be very aware of propriety. It is inappropriate for Miss Kenton, the housekeeper, to address the under-butler as "William," even though she is his superior. And, just to let Stevens know she's no fool, and that his father's work is not quite up to par, she tells him that the Chinaman statue that used to be on the upstairs landing is now downstairs by the billiard room. Cleary the under-butler, Stevens' father, is not doing his job well, and Miss Kenton believes Stevens should know. But the Chinaman represents far more than just a statue out of place. Miss Kenton then explains the subtext she's been trying to get across.

> MISS KENTON
> Your father is entrusted with more than
> a man of his age can cope with.

And she's right. He soon gets more and more frail and ill, and then dies. The use of the words "of his age" and "cope" foreshadow the father's death.

In *Psycho*, the word "trap" is used to evoke meaning. Mary says she "stepped into a private trap." Later, it's clear she has stepped into a far deeper trap than she expected.

Norman Bates talks about "habits," a word that describes patterns and ritual responses, as well as the clothes that we wear, which is, of course, suggestive of the "habit" or disguise he puts on when he impersonates his mother. The word implies both meanings.

Norman Bates talks about the "formalities" of lighting the motel sign even though no one ever stops at the motel anymore. Norman is someone who keeps up appearances and formalities: He keeps going, just as before, even though many things have changed. He keeps acting as if his mother is alive, even though she's dead. He keeps acting as if nothing is wrong at the motel, even though a lot is.

REPEATING A WORD FOR FURTHER RESONANCE

Sometimes a word is repeated several times. The subtext comes out not just through the individual word but also through the repetition of it. In *Ordinary People*, the whole family is suffering, trying to cope with the death of the older son. Yet, it takes some time for anyone in the family to admit he or she is suffering. The word "great," emphasized a number of times, shows this denial. When Conrad tells his father his friend is picking him up to take him to school, Calvin says, "Oh, is he? Great!" Conrad questions, "Why is it great?" When the grandmother is ready to take a photo of the family, she's says, "That's great," as they move closer together. Even Grandfather thinks "it's great." At a party, Calvin is asked how Conrad is doing and he replies, "He's great. Just great." When Karen asks Conrad about his swimming, she assures him, "You'll do great." He calls her later and leaves the message with her parents that he's "feeling great." She suggests they have a "great Christmas," which she doesn't, since she commits suicide.

Characters also repeat words about loss. Calvin talks to Beth about his client who "lost everything." Calvin's jogging partner comments on how Calvin gets lost in his thoughts: "I've been losing you these days." *Ordinary People* is a story about loss, and reinvoking these few words reinforces that theme.

The film *Shadow of Doubt* is about a man who kills many people. The word "kill" is repeated several times. At one point, Mrs. Newton says:

> MRS. NEWTON
> Charles, you're going to kill me
> when you hear what I've done.

> UNCLE CHARLIE
> Emmy, I'd never kill you no matter
> what you've done.

And that's the truth, although there is more truth — he has killed others, but he wouldn't kill her.

USING INNUENDO

Innuendo is often used when someone is not allowed to speak the truth outright. This obscuring is sometimes used in a sexual

64

context: "Would you like to come upstairs — perhaps for a little something?" She's probably not talking about coffee or a drink. Innuendo is also used in spy stories, or stories about undercover cops, or political or corruption stories where there's danger. The truth is then disguised and implied, rather than said outright.

The play and film *Doubt* (2008, by John Patrick Shanley) concerns the doubt Sister Aloysius (Meryl Streep) has about Father Flynn, the priest at their church and school. She begins to plant the seeds of doubt when talking to the other nuns during dinner.

SISTER ALOYSIUS
I am concerned, perhaps needlessly,
about, eh, matters in St. Nicholas School.

She has protected herself by saying "needlessly," but she's also implied a number of possibilities by the word "matters." As the film proceeds, we see what "matters" are on her mind.

In *Valkyrie* (2008, by Christopher McQuarrie) Colonel Claus von Stauffenberg (Tom Cruise) is part of a group planning to assassinate Hitler. Colonel Stauffenberg meets with Friedrich Fromm (Tom Wilkinson) who, he believes, might also be critical of the Hitler regime and thus be willing to join their group. It's dangerous to ask him outright so he uses innuendo. Instead of asking for his help, he discusses the subject of making decisions.

FROMM
They tell me you're critical of the war.

Well, maybe he is also — but Stauffenberg is not sure.

STAUFFENBERG
I'm critical of indecision.

That's why he's here — hoping Fromm will make a decision — will he join them? Will he help them?

FROMM
So, that's why you're here... to make decisions.

```
                    STAUFFENBERG
     I've already made my decision. I'm here to help others
                      make theirs.
```

"Others," meaning, of course, Fromm.

```
                        FROMM
     They say when there's no clear option, the best thing
                      is to do nothing.
```

Is Fromm testing Stauffenberg? Or is he recommending no-body do anything? Stauffenberg, once again, uses innuendo to try to find out.

```
                    STAUFFENBERG
     We're at war. We must act, sometimes rashly.
```

The action being planned is rash. Is he with them, or not?

```
                        FROMM
     What rash action did you have in mind, Colonel?
```

He's trying to get more information.

```
                    STAUFFENBERG
     That would be a decision for the Supreme Military Commander.
```

Such as yourself — where do you stand?

```
                        FROMM
     I don't need to remind you that we've all sworn an oath
                      to the Führer.
```

This conversation is getting too dangerous. On the other hand, Fromm seems to have enough sympathy for Stauffenberg not to turn him in — although nothing specific has been done where a law has been broken or disloyalty has clearly been shown. He disconnects the phone.

```
     Having said that, I'm going to forget this discussion
     ever took place. You can tell your friends, Colonel,
                      that I always
         come down on the right side and as long as the
         Führer is alive, you know what side that is.
                      Heil Hitler.
```

He's making it clear — "I won't join you," but by disconnecting the phone, he's also makes clear he's not going to report him. Some of the danger has been removed.

TALKING ABOUT ONE THING, MEANING ANOTHER

Sometimes a character talks about a subject that seems to have nothing to do with the current topic. If the writer has chosen the words carefully, we understand what is really being said.

In *Shadow of Doubt*, Young Charlie has fallen in love with Jack. Jack is a detective who has been working on the black widow murder case, in which her uncle is a suspect. When it seems that Uncle Charlie is probably innocent, Jack says he has to leave since there's no longer a reason to stay and investigate further. Young Charlie admits she doesn't want him to go, but instead of talking about not wanting him to go, or talking about how she's fallen in love with him, she talks about her mother's lost glove. She goes on and on, talking about how her mother is "always losing something." Why is Young Charlie suddenly talking about a lost glove? What is she really talking about? She's talking about her own sense of loss. She's talking about how she fears she will lose him, just as her mother lost her glove. She might be talking about how others have become lost to her — such as her Uncle Charlie. With this kind of dialogue we often think, "Why in the world is she talking about this?" The subject of the dialogue doesn't seem to relate to anything. But the words have been clearly chosen and, as a result, we get the subtext.

USING A DOUBLE ENTENDRE

One of the easiest and most-overused methods for getting at subtext is through double entendre. The words refer to one thing, but the underlying meaning of the words signals back to sexuality, or body parts, or bathroom activities. Often the joke is childish, referring back to those days when one wasn't

supposed to use "those words," so the words had to be disguised. 67
The reaction to the joke is often a giggle or a smirk or a snort
that says, "I can't believe you said that out loud!" As a result,
the double entendre easily becomes cheap and is used mainly to
gross out the audience.

However, if used sparingly, double entendre can be effective.
In *Revolutionary Road*, after April's husband has taken their neighbor Millie home from a dance, April turns to Shepp, Millie's
husband, and says "Let's do it!" seemingly referring to dancing
but really referring to having sex. April is flirtatious, seductive,
seemingly wild and free, and after dancing together, they "do
it" in the car.

In *Psycho*, Mary says: "I'm going to spend this weekend in bed,"
meaning she's tired and wants to rest. Cassidy changes the meaning
of the word and says, "Only playground that beats Las Vegas!"

Sometimes the double entendre is used as a private communication between two people, so that only they understand. If
two parents are thinking of sex after dinner, they might say, "I
can hardly wait for dessert." As the children shout "yippee!"
the parents wink at each other. They're clear about their real
meaning.

Although this method can be too repetitive, too on-the-nose,
and too much of a cliché, there are still fresh ways of showing
attraction and desire. Occasionally a film or television series
uses double entendre cleverly without getting cheap but rather
to explore character and situation.

In *The Big Sleep*, Philip Marlowe (Humphrey Bogart) and Mrs.
Rutledge (Lauren Bacall) talk about the horse races, but they're
really talking about their sexual attraction to each other.
Marlowe is finishing up a case for Mrs. Rutledge's father, and
these two have clearly been attracted to each other from the
beginning of the case.

68

> MRS. RUTLEDGE
> Tell me, what do you usually do when you're
> not working?

Sounds like she's interested in his off-work time.

> MARLOWE
> Play the horses, fool around...

"Fool around" — a carefully chosen phrase suggesting he'd be willing to fool around with her.

> MRS. RUTLEDGE
> Well, speaking of horses, I like to play them myself.

Yes, she's ready, willing, and able. But lest he think she's a bit too easy, she has her own ideas about how these things should work.

> But I like to see them work out a little
> first. See if they're front runners or come from
> behind. Find out... what makes them run.

She has herself figured out, but she also has him figured out.

> I'd say you don't like to be rated.

"Rating a horse" means holding him back, or keeping him from running full out. She knows this is not a man you try to control.

> You like to get out
> in front, open up a lead, take a
> little breather in the back stretch, and then
> come home free.

Marlowe is a man who needs a certain amount of freedom. He runs his own race, and you don't try to change that.

> MARLOWE
> You don't like to be rated yourself.

> MRS. RUTLEDGE
> I haven't met anyone yet who
> can do it. Any suggestions?

She's open to the possibility of someone having a bit of control over her, but so far, she hasn't met anyone who can do it to her satisfaction.

> MARLOWE
> Well, I can't tell till I've seen you
> over a distance of ground. You got a touch
> of class, but I don't know how far you can go.

Certainly he'll know more if it's not just a one-night stand. How might this relationship look over a period of time?

> RUTLEDGE
> A lot depends on who's in the saddle!...

Usually, the person driving the relationship is not someone she wants driving her. She's not someone who likes to be reined in, but then, that depends on the rider! Some rein in and it feels good!

> MARLOWE
> There's one thing I can't quite figure out.

> RUTLEDGE
> What makes me run?... I'll give you a
> little hint - sugar won't work, it's been tried...
> Simply sweet talking and wine and roses won't work!

> MARLOWE
> Who told you to sugar me off this case?

And now they're back to the text about the case.

In the long-running series, *Cheers* (created by Les and Glen Charles and James Burrows), Dr. Frasier Crane (Kelsey Grammer) an eminent psychiatrist in the Boston area who spends time in the Cheers bar, meets Dr. Lilith Sternin (Bebe Neuwirth). They have an antagonistic relationship toward each other, which turns into a love relationship in the fifth season.

In the episode called "Abnormal Psychology" (by Janet Leahy), Frasier is asked to be a guest on a television interview show, but when he hears that Dr. Sternin is the other guest, he intends to cancel. He doesn't like her and most of the others in the bar know this, although as the episode develops, we realize the real subtext.

When Frasier mentions Lilith Sternin, Carla interprets the subtext about why Frasier wants to cancel his appearance on the show.

                    CARLA
          Can't handle debating a woman, eh?

Frasier denies her interpretation.

                    FRASIER
          A woman, yes. An iceberg in heels, no.
    Look, I have no intention of entering a debate with those
        cold gray eyes and those clever smirking lips.
            I'd rather clip my nails in a cuisinart.

Just when we are very clear Frasier dislikes this woman, Diane interprets the true meaning of Frasier's words, telling us the subtext that is not clear to anyone else in the bar. As usual, she's right.

                    DIANE
                  Oh, my...

Sam, who has no ability to read subtext unless it's clearly sexual, is very confused over Diane's reaction.

                    SAM
                What's wrong?

                    DIANE
        Oh, don't you see? Frasier's in love...

We might be wondering how Diane would know to discern this subtext when Frasier's words clearly belie this interpretation. But Diane continues, clarifying how she knows this interpretation is, in fact, the meaning of the subtext.

```
                    DIANE
      You're forgetting I was once romantically
   involved with Frasier. I know when he's enamored
    with someone. Didn't you see his nostrils flare?
```

Ah, she interprets his romantic interest by this very subtle change in his facial muscles. Okay, maybe we'll buy that, but we need more proof of her interpretation. Diane then tries to explain to Sam how one can say one thing and really mean the opposite.

```
                    DIANE
      ... Quite often you expressed feelings of
        antagonism toward me and we both know
                 how much you love me.
```

At this point in the series and in the episode, we're not sure Diane's interpretation is correct, although as the episode develops, we'll see that Diane, once more, is right.

But Frasier has another interpretation — sometimes what people say is exactly what they mean — there isn't always subtext.

```
                   FRASIER
      Believe it or not, Sam, it's actually
   possible to have hostile feelings toward someone
            without being in love with them.
```

```
                     SAM
      You mean I can actually hate Diane without
     having it mean anything more than I hate her?
```

```
                   FRASIER
                  Feel free.
```

So, the text might mean exactly what it says, except in this case, that's not true.

Lilith comes to confront Frasier and suggest they set down some ground rules. He agrees. After Frasier leaves, Diane interprets the subtext to Lilith, telling her she believes these hostile feelings from Frasier are really masking a "deep-seated attraction" to her, an interpretation Lilith doesn't believe either. Diane also volunteers to help Lilith with her hair and make-up before the show, which might give her an advantage on television. She agrees. Diane transforms Lilith into a somewhat ravishing brunette, which clearly has an effect on Frasier during the interview.

Lilith enters the interview, taking her seat on the other side of the host. All Frasier can do is stare — and stare some more. Obviously she's beautiful and he's noticing.

The host asks Frasier to describe his method of working with the patient's psyche. Clearly, as Frasier answers, he is thinking about Lilith, not his method of psychological treatment.

FRASIER
My method of flooding seeks out the
patient's most sensitive and vulnerable spot
in the defense system and penetrates,
probing deeper and deeper into the patient's psyche,
thrusting over and over and thereby uncovering
the reality behind the irrational fear.

The host doesn't exactly know what to make of this, but says "Thank You," with a bit of a catch in his voice. He then turns to Dr. Sternin for her response. She describes her approach. As with Frasier, the response isn't about pure psychology.

LILITH
... Although Dr. Crane's method is faster,
a slow and methodical approach can be much more
rewarding. Gentle stroking of the psyche can bring about
a far more and intense release of emotion,
building until the patient quite often will literally
cry out in a release of satisfaction and joy.

FRASIER
Point well taken.

And just in case we missed the point — how could we? — we see Sam and Diane, clutching each other's hands, hot and bothered by all this psychology. At the end of the TV show, as the host tells the audience where they can get a transcript of this interview, Frasier and Lilith play footsie. As the episode proceeds, we see Frasier is clearly embarrassed by his behavior, as he tells his friends at the bar.

> FRASIER
> The only consolation is that nobody ever
> watches that show.

Just then, a man walks past and tells Frasier, "Way to go, sex machine!" Obviously, others caught the subtext.

Still, Frasier doesn't understand the extent of his attraction to Lilith. When Lilith returns to the bar to apologize for her behavior, and their antagonism comes out again, Diane comes to the rescue. She tells Lilith the refrigerator door is stuck again and they need a hairpin. Clearly, she's hoping that if Lilith lets down her hair again, Frasier will respond. He does. The two leave the bar together, going to Frasier's "tastefully decorated apartment" to stop being so logical and be the animals they'd like to be — at least for a while.

PLAYING WITH DOUBLE MEANINGS OF WORDS

Just as the *Cheers* episode plays with the double meaning of words such as "thrusting" and "stroking," writers sometimes use a word in a nonsexual way, conveying two different meanings for the same word. The first time we hear the word, we are probably thinking (consciously or unconsciously) of the second meaning.

In *Psycho*, Sam gets coffee for Lisa, and says:

> SAM
> It's regular. Okay?

Lisa responds, clearly tired of all the irregular and abnormal things that have been going on:

> LISA
> I could stand something regular.

In *As Good as it Gets*, Carol's fellow waitresses offer to loan her money for a cab so she can get home early to get ready for her date. Carol replies, "Ready is not my problem!" This simple line implies that Carol hasn't had a date for some time. Later, she tells Melvin he's "not ready," and since she knows the difference between being ready and not being ready, she's quite right.

The word "ready" is used to imply similar meaning in *The Big Sleep*. Mrs. Rutledge is ready to gamble at roulette, and then she intends to get a ride home from Philip Marlowe. As the owner of the establishment is ready to spin the wheel, she's asked, "Are you ready?" She replies, "Yes, I'm ready." Her answer resonates on three levels. She's ready to have the wheel spun. She's ready to get a ride with Marlowe. And she's ready for the relationship with Marlowe that's been brewing for some time.

In *Valkyrie*, as Colonel von Stauffenberg is in a private room preparing the bomb, his aide tells the S.S. Guard who's knocking at the door, "The Colonel is changing. You understand this can be difficult." The aide uses the word "difficult" to imply that the Colonel has difficulty changing because of his amputated hand and fingers and it would be embarrassing if he were observed by the guard. The aide hopes the guard understands his usage of the word in that way, which he does, and leaves the Colonel alone. But we know the real meaning of the word — Stauffenberg is having difficulty preparing the bomb and putting all the pieces together.

TALKING ABOUT ONE THING, MEANING ANOTHER

Subtext is often revealed when a character seemingly talks about one thing, but is really addressing something quite different. In *Sideways* (2004, by Alexander Payne and Jim Taylor, from the novel by Rex Pickett), Maya and Miles talk about why they love wine, but they're really talking about themselves and their attitudes toward life. Maya asks Miles why he has such a thing about Pinot Noir. His answer tells us much about his attitude toward himself.

>   MILES
>   It needs constant care and attention...
>   And only the most patient and nurturing growers can...
>   tap into Pinot's most fragile, delicate qualities.

He also adds that he thinks Cabernet is prosaic, and it's clear Miles does not want to be thought of as prosaic.

Maya explains that she loves "how wine continues to evolve." But Maya also knows that when it peaks, like a love relationship, wine can begin its "steady, inevitable decline." She knows things are peaking with Miles, but not sure he'll know when to open up to possibilities.

In some murder stories, the villain reveals his murder plans in subtext, while talking about something quite different.

In *Shadow of Doubt*, Uncle Charlie tells us about how to give a good speech, but he's really talking about his method of killing women.

>   UNCLE CHARLIE
>   You've got to make a plan. Think of
>   every detail of what you're going to
>   say or do. Nothing in the world is
>   difficult if you plan ahead. ...
>   Then when you've planned everything to
>   the last detail, forget it until the
>   moment arrives. Use the moment when it
>   comes. Don't keep turning it over in your
>   mind beforehand... or after... Soon, it's
>   all over, and you'll be thinking of
>   other things.

The description can give clues to the readers, producer, director, and art directors about the subtext, and about the shading that needs to come across in other ways besides dialogue. In the opening scene of *Psycho*, Sam tries to raise the shade, but it sticks and comes down, "and the hot sun glares into the room, revealing it in all its shabbiness and sordidness." As the story develops, we realize Mary's life is shabby and sordid and has reached a breaking point and a finishing point.

Later there's a description of Norman's parlor, "Lit only by the light from the office spilling in." Blood spills as well as light. The description of the walls in the room is equally suggestive: "Fat roses splatter the wallpaper." The use of the word "splatter" is clearly preparing us for the splattering of blood when Mary is killed in the shower.

In *Doubt*, Sister Aloysius talks to Sister James about a student named Noreen, who has been wearing a very fancy barrette. It just won't do. As Sister Aloysius takes the barrette and opens it to examine it, the description says, "It looks like little legs spreading." Sister Aloysius then reinforces the idea by telling Sister James, "Just get her through. Intact."

In *Ordinary People*, when "Beth prepares the table geometrically," we receive a telling detail that conveys how Beth wants everything to be perfect.

In *Remains of the Day*, Stevens meets Miss Kenton years later and has tea with her. As they're ready to go, the description mentions "the remains of the tea on the table," like the remains of their relationship. In case we missed the point, the last scene takes place in the evening, with Stevens sitting on a bench looking out to sea. A man sitting next to him points out: "The evening's the best part of the day." Stevens has once more said goodbye to bringing love into his life. He thinks he has nothing else to give and is too old and that Miss Kenton has other plans anyway. But the man articulates, metaphorically, that evening is still a very good time.

CHOOSING NAMES

Names can also imply subtext that helps deepen the character. In *Witness*, the main character is named John Book — he's honest and does things by the book. In *Psycho*, the character who gets killed is named Mary Crane, like the bird. In one scene, she sits in Norman's parlor, taking little bird-bites of her food, while staring at the stuffed dead birds that decorate the room. Soon, Mary Crane is dead as well.

Jack Sparrow in *Pirates of the Caribbean* (2003, 2006, 2007) moves like a sparrow, quickly flitting in and out. Hannibal Lector lectures Starling about the darkness of human nature, and shows the darkness through his character. Gilbert Grape in *What's Eating Gilbert Grape* (1993) is innocent, plump, slightly touched by the magic of the sun.

Breakfast at Tiffany's (1961) has a main character named Holly Golightly, a charming girl who walks lightly through life. *The Messenger* has two main characters — one is named "Will," who shows moments of being willful; the other is Captain Stone — hard, unemotional, but solid like a rock. He follows his orders and does everything by the rules.

Revolutionary Road has two main characters, Frank and April Wheeler. Wheels are what we usually ride on when we're going places, and the Wheelers want to go to Paris, but their dreams are stopped in their tracks. April is a name suggesting spring, hope, new beginnings, but April will also be stopped in her tracks by her husband's decision to follow the conventional route, and by her pregnancy, which she decides to abort. In so doing, she goes against her name — instead of reinforcing new beginnings, she neither gets the baby, which is the new life, nor gets Paris. And she loses her own life in the process.

Creative naming need not only apply to people's names, it may also apply to towns, hotels, or places. The hotel in *Casino Royale* is named Hotel Splendide. In the film, Bond announces to Vesper that they'll be using names other than their own. She will be named "Miss Stephanie Broadchest."

In *Avatar*, the mountains are floating and their name is, aptly, "The Hallelujah Mountains."

CREATING METAPHORS THROUGH THE TITLE

Some films create metaphors through their titles. *Revolutionary Road* is about a neighborhood that is anything but revolutionary. It takes place in the unrevolutionary 1950s, when women and men abided by what was appropriate.

The film *Chocolat* (2000) plays with our associations with chocolate. For many of us, chocolate is about joy, the deliciousness of life, and sometimes being just a bit on the edge of what's proper if we eat too much of it. Chocolate is about being spontaneous and engaging with others versus being rigid and self-disciplined. The story involves a woman named Vianne Rocher (Juliet Binoche) and her young daughter who move to a town in rural France and open up a chocolate store across the street from a church. The mayor doesn't welcome their arrival one bit. If there was ever a man in need of chocolate, it's the mayor. His life is neither rich nor sweet. The story is about rules set against that which is delicious in our lives – love, humor, sweetness, spontaneity, tenderness, interaction. Rules can't contain our yearning for life to be yummy – even when rulers, of one sort or another, try.

The title of the *The Reader* (2008) tells us what the story is about – a boy who reads to a woman. But, of course, it's about far more. The title also tells us about the subtext. If you were to brainstorm thirty or even fifty associations you have with reading, you might mention that reading brings us into other worlds,

introduces us to new realities, helps us to imagine other possibilities or to escape our own lives. Reading allows us to walk in
the shoes of another, to see through the eyes of another, to feel
another's emotions, to understand another's perspective.

In *The Reader*, we see a woman who is ashamed of her inability
of read, which relates to her inability to understand basic human interactions and the emotions of others. She is ashamed
of something she can't define, which has to do with her inability
to be empathic. Yet she clearly yearns for this connection. We
might say the movie is partly about shame. Hanna might feel the
barest twinges of it and know, or sense, that she's missing some
ingredient that is basic to humanity.

If we analyze Hanna, we see she is a person with a very narrow
view of the world. She can't see through the eyes of another. At
the trial, it's clear that she lacks empathy — the ability to understand and feel another's point of view. She's trapped by rules
and commands, by rituals and order, by living only by the rules
of her immediate context. So we see a character who, on some
unconscious level, wants the world of books. On some unconscious level, she wants to overcome her isolation. On some
unconscious level, she wants reading to help her to escape her
narrow world.

Slumdog Millionaire (2008) is a basic contradiction in terms. Its
title implies the film's contrasts between the oppressed and
powerful, the poor and the rich, the haves and have-nots, the
abused and the abusers. The title carries associations with social
issues of which we might already be aware — issues relating to
racism, sexism, and classism. The story explores the contrasts
and disparities, and the hope of moving from an oppressed
state to a freer, more liberated life.

Blindside (2009) evokes notions of protection, of how people
take care of each other, even when weak, and protect those vulnerable places that we can't see clearly. It also suggests being hit,
literally or metaphorically, by surprise,

Avatar (2009, by James Cameron) plays with the different mean-ings of its title. In Hinduism, avatar refers to the incarnation or manifestation of a deity. It carries meanings of "crossing over" or descending into physical form. Sometimes the deity takes a human form, or the form of an animal, such as a fish, tortoise, or boar. The word is also used in computer games. "In works of New Media, an avatar is a visual image on the screen that rep-resents the player," says New Media expert, Carolyn Handler Miller. She continues:

> The player can control the avatar and make it speak and perform all kinds of actions. Avatars can "die" and they can also increase in strength and skill level. They can communicate and interact with other avatars. In many cases, the players can construct their avatars out of a num-ber of choices, picking their facial features, body types, hair color and so on. In some cases, avatars can be actual physical constructs such as robots. The avatar may represent the user's actions, belief systems, social status, background, emotions, or interests. In some cases, as with on screen representa-tions, these physical avatars act as "stand ins" for the players and are controlled by them. They can move around in the real world, lift their "arms" and talk.

In *Avatar*, because they are unable to breathe the air on Pandora, humans take the form of genetically bred Na'vi hybrids, known as avatars. These avatars are controlled by the humans through a technology that links the human's mind to the body of the avatar, which now has a new form as a Na'vi. Although Jake is unable to walk as a human, he is able to walk and run as an avatar.

Jake has, in the Hindu sense, descended into a new form, be-coming a new person, with a new identity, in a new community. It is implied, according to the humans, that he has moved from a higher stage, to a lower stage, just as the deity takes a lesser form by taking on a physical form. Yet, as the movie proceeds, the earthlings seem to be the less enlightened form, and the Na'vis seem more in harmony, more enlightened, and more collaborative in the way they relate to each other.

Avatar deploys another word to evoke subtextual meanings — through "Pandora," the name of the planet. Many will think of the association with "Pandora's Box," the story of Pandora, who opened up a box allowing all sorts of evil to escape. The name implies something that looks pleasant and nonthreatening, but when opened has unforeseen, dire consequences. In this case, opening up the planet of Pandora lets loose new possibilities for Jake, and dire consequences for humans. There is a choice — whether to open the box and, if so, whether to side with the humans who want to conquer and destroy, or the Na'vis, who want to preserve. In the myth of Pandora's Box, one item was left after all the evils had been loosed — Hope.

In 2009, another one-word title filled with subtext was *Invictus*. The word comes from the Latin word "invincible," "uncon-quered," or "undefeated." The title of the movie is taken from the title of a poem, written in 1875 by William Ernest Henley shortly before his leg was amputated. The poem contains many images of being unbowed: "under the bludgeoning of chance my head is bloody, but unbowed." And the poem ends, "I am the master of my fate, I am the captain of my soul." Although many audiences may not know the poem, the title might evoke the feeling of invincibility that inspired the South African Rugby team to win the World Cup as South Africa was moving from apartheid to reconciliation between whites and blacks.

Any of these allusions can emerge intuitively. Many times, the title will be chosen in the rewrite process, as the writer works at putting text into subtext.

QUESTIONS TO ASK OF YOUR SCRIPT

(1) Look at a scene from your script where you feel you've incorporated subtext well. Make two columns: title one "text" and the other "subtext." Or, you might decide to write out the subtext underneath the text, as I've done in various examples above. If there's no subtext, then go back and rewrite the scene. Notice if you've naturally used any of these techniques in your script. Could you use others?

(2) Watch some films that are filled with subtext, such as *Remains of the Day*, *Ordinary People*, *American Beauty*, or a Hitchcock film. Watch a section, and then stop the film and ask: "What is really going on here? How is the subtext expressed?"

(3) You might want to buy the Season Five episodes of *Cheers* (available on DVD) and watch the "Abnormal Psychology" episode. These episodes offer some of the best examples of subtext and are worthy of study. How many examples of subtext can you find?

(4) Watch some of your favorite television shows and see how many examples of subtext you can find. You might choose shows such as *Damages*, *Big Love*, *Weeds*, or *Lost*, which deal with what is unseen and unspoken. Listen for subtext in sit-coms and television movies. What techniques are used to get at the subtext?

(5) Look at your own script. How deep is the character? How layered? Have you grounded the character in subtext and implied any character traits and attitudes without talking about them?

expressing subtext through gestures and action

Much of the subtext is revealed through actions that characters take, whether simple gestures or playing out the big events in the story. The gestures and action tell the truth, even if the words lie.

Subtext is especially important in film, because what we see tells us a world of truth about a character. In novels, we can learn the truth about a character through what the character says (provided the character isn't lying to us), what the character does (provided the character isn't putting on an act), what others say about the character (which may or may not be a lie), and what the narrator tells us (provided the narrator is reliable). In a novel, the narrator is often the truth-teller. If the truth isn't clear through the character's words and actions, the narrator can tell us the subtext, sometimes interrupting the story to clarify the meaning.

In film everything needs to be revealed through words, sounds, and visuals. Even if a voice over tries to tell us the truth, we won't believe it unless it is confirmed by what we see.

84   LOOK AT THE GESTURES

If we're unsure about the truth, we can look to a character's gestures. Although some gestures will be motivated by the actor, it isn't unusual for a writer to write: "She picks up her handkerchief delicately," or "He cleans his gun methodically," or "He leans back, looking up at the stars." The smaller movements can be as telling as the larger actions. The truth is often in the details.

Sometimes the gestures directly contradict the words. In *Shadow of Doubt*, a detective is searching for Uncle Charlie. Although Uncle Charlie acts nonchalant about his presence, he shows the threat he feels through his gestures: "Uncle Charlie... clutches his napkin with his fist."

Uncle Charlie starts "to unwind the wire from the neck of the bottle.... with meticulous care," almost as if he's strangling someone — which he has done in the past.

Later, in a scene in a bar with his niece, Uncle Charlie "takes one paper napkin after another — twists them and throws them on the floor."

Tension builds. Uncle Charlie is no longer so unflappable.

Sometimes the gesture is unconscious. If Uncle Charlie consciously noticed what he was doing, he might try to stop himself. In fact, when Young Charlie calls attention to what he's doing, Uncle Charlie realizes it and stops.

Sometimes it's unclear whether a character is doing a gesture on purpose. Are the gestures unconscious or conscious?

Emma Newton, Uncle Charlie's sister, would like a little extra attention from her husband. As she prepares for bed, "she runs her fingers down the side of her neck, then opens the top of her nightdress a little... she removes the shade from the table light.

The added light makes her appear almost youthful — she smiles

happily."

Emma then tries words to call her husband's attention to her beauty. She hopes if the gestures don't work, the subject matter will.

```
                    MRS. NEWTON
        46 Burnham Street... the prettiest girl
        in the block... I was the prettiest girl
                    in the block.
```

Subtext makes us ask "Why"? Why is she bringing up this subject about the past at this time? And then we think, "Oh, I understand. She wants him to notice that she's pretty, and sexually attractive, and therefore get him to respond." She never says as much, but it's clear from the overall context.

When subtext is implied, we ask questions. We become like a detective, or a dog with a bone, gleefully chewing on the implied question and seeing beneath the talk and the actions.

In *Revolutionary Road*, when April appears to have accepted the fact they aren't going to Paris and that she'll need to make the best of the situation and be a good wife, she asks Frank whether he wants his eggs fried or scrambled. As a writer, you might ask, "What would be the best answer to convey the subtext of the moment?" You might think about the associations with "fried." You might think about how April's brain is "fried" by the situation. But, it also might be a metaphor without much dramatic mileage. Frank chooses "scrambled." This choice provides more subtext. Their lives are scrambled and mixed up. The scrambled eggs also have a sexual and reproductive overtone. His choice also gives April the opportunity to scramble eggs in a frenetic manner that belies the "happy housewife" look she's trying to project.

In *Casablanca*, Renault (the police chief played by Claude Raines) tosses a bottle of Vichy water into the trash. In the backstory (and in history), the French Vichy government collaborated with the Nazis. By tossing the Vichy bottle, Renault implies that he is no longer going to collaborate, he is switching his loyalty to Rick and Victor Laszlo.

LOOK AT BODY LANGUAGE

Some years ago, a friend was romantically interested in one of her colleagues. They knew each other, but they weren't dating. She invited him to a dinner party, along with my husband and me and a few other friends. We all knew of her interest and were wondering if he would ask her out at the end of the evening. After he left the dinner party, several of us remained and discussed the possibility of romance. My husband, who has always been very good at reading people, told her with great confidence, "He won't ask you out." When she asked why, he explained the subtext in his body language. "Did you notice when he sat next to you, his shoulders were turned away from you, and his legs were crossed away from you, blocking you out? Although he was nice and good company, there was no real interest in you." Peter was right. Our friend went on to happily marry someone else, who didn't block her out.

We see subtext all around us. We should be able to remove the words and read the body language, in real life or in film. What do certain physical behaviors really mean? In the 2010 Olympics, two male ice skaters were favored to win the gold for men's figure skating — Evgeni Plushenko from Russia and Evan Lysacek from the United States. Evgeni was one of the few skaters able to do quadruple jumps, but Evan had more complex choreography and, many commentators said, more artistry. When Evan won by 1.86 points, Evgeni was clearly angry — in fact, all of Russia seemed angry, believing the gold was rightfully his. How did he show it? Through his body language. As soon as the gold medalist was announced, Evgeni walked quickly away. When it came time to mount the podium, he did something highly unusual: He walked to his second place position on the podium by walking onto the gold medal position first, and then moving over to his designated place as the silver medal winner. Although he smiled and pretended it was a joke, it clearly was not — he felt his rightful place was as a Gold Medal Winner, and he wanted to stand there.

Where else do we see subtext? A woman who keeps opening up her blouse a bit, or unbuttoning the top button, is sending a message that is probably very clear if there's a man nearby. Of course, if it's in the tropics and very hot and she's alone, her action may mean nothing more than she's warm and trying to cool off a bit.

Sometimes people speak with their hand over their mouth. Does this mean they're insecure? Or, really don't want people listening to them? Or, aren't sure about what they're saying?

Perhaps a woman crosses her legs and arms. Even though she might say she's open to a relationship, we know she's closed. Or, she uncrosses her legs, as in *Basic Instinct* (1992), and tells the men in the room there are possibilities — taunting them at the same time.

One of my friends told me her brother used to walk five steps ahead of his siblings when he walked to school, indicating his desire to disassociate from the family. As life went on, that subtext continued to clarify itself.

Sometimes before people commit suicide, they first hold the gun or clean the gun or look at the gun. Although they might deny what they're thinking, the subtext seems absolutely clear. The body language tells us there's a threat and real danger here.

This threat may also be directed outward. If a gun is pointed directly at you, it's a good idea to take it seriously and not insert a James Bond quip or believe any comforting line the person holding the gun tells you. You may not live long enough to develop your ability to read a situation.

People sometimes make outward gestures that imply inward changes. In *As Good as it Gets*, Melvin always goes to "his" restaurant at the same time, has the same waitress, and sits at the same table. But, as he begins to make some inner changes, he changes his table. The simple move from one table to another tells us a world about what's really going on. Melvin changes his table so that he can watch the dog. But beneath the surface, if we asked what's really going on, we would answer, "He's taken a baby step to begin changing his life!" The change of table means far more than simply sitting somewhere else to catch a better view.

That's what we do in real life. Perhaps we choose one table over another because we want a better view, or to see the TV, or to sit at the more romantic table with candlelight and low lighting. And we usually tell the maitre d' the truth — without subtext: "Oh, the view is beautiful! Could we have the table by the window so we can see the Hills of Rome from here?" (This remark, of course, assumes we are in Rome and not just thinking we are. In the latter case, the subtext would concern delusion and madness).

Or, the husband tells the maitre d', "It's our wedding anniversary and we'd love that romantic table in the corner, with the soft candlelight." There'd be no subtext, unless the husband wanted the dark corner so nobody would see him slip the poison into his wife's drink and then, as the story proceeds, inherit all her money.

Or, you might tell the maitre d', "I'd like to sit at the table with more light, so I can do some work while I'm eating. I have a big meeting tomorrow and still need to prepare." And, that's probably the truth, unless you're really asking for the well-lit table so the handsome man without the wedding ring sitting catty-corner will see you. You sit down at the table with the most flattering light, slip off your wedding ring under the table, drop it in your purse, proceed to put the work aside and swirl your almost empty glass of wine, occasionally making eye contact. You're hoping he'll notice. If your subtext is successful, the waiter will come over to your table and let you know the man over there would like to buy you a drink. You'll say "yes," and beckon him to join you, telling him you just wanted to thank him (but knowing that's not what's going on at all). Then more subtext will unfold as you strategize the next moves.

LOOK AT THE CHARACTER'S RHYTHM AND PACE

People tell us about a situation by their pace and rhythm. Do they act quickly? With energy? Or are they slow as a turtle? People can show subtext by being fast in their actions — as if they want to get something over with quickly or are running from something. They can move slowly in order to control another person. Or they might linger, enjoying every moment. If depressed, they might shuffle and walk with their eyes downcast.

In 1993, I went on a horseback riding vacation in France with two friends. My friend Carol was extremely good at reading people and situations. The leader of the group, Paul, was having an affair with a woman from Germany, who had been with him the first day, and was returning to see him on Thursday. She would be spending the evening with us, and, we presumed, the night with him. As we rode our horses back to the inn, we all knew she'd be waiting for him when we arrived. And she was. As the evening went on, however, I noticed that although the sweet mistress was dressed up and clearly interested in Paul, he didn't seem to be as interested in her as one might expect. At the end of the evening, Carol supplied the complete story of the subtext. She began:

Did you notice that the closer we got to the B & B, the slower Paul rode? Horses will usually pick up their speed a bit as they get closer to food and rest, but Paul was clearly slowing down until we were going at a snail's pace. He was not interested in seeing her. She is the one pushing this relationship. Did you notice how pretty she looked? She wore a special dress and was the only one of us dressed up. She sat turned toward him all during dinner, and he kept averting his eyes and turning away.

And Carol added, "I felt sorry for her, since this was a lost cause and she may not know it yet."

We all became aware Paul seemed more relaxed after she left. And, like many of us who might have once been in a similar situation, we wondered how long it would take for her to read the subtext.

LOOK AT HABITUAL BEHAVIORS

Many people have behaviors that are clearly habits, often bad habits. Sometimes habitual behavior becomes a mental disorder. In *As Good as it Gets*, Melvin has an obsessive-compulsive disorder that causes him to lock and unlock the door five times before he feels he's safely inside. He also throws out his germ-laden gloves and then washes his hands with two kinds of soap. His gestures and actions clearly indicate behavior that is part of the disorder. So, the text simply proves that there is a mental disorder. But there is also a subtextual level to Melvin's actions. The particular ailment the writers chose has a deeper meaning: It's a metaphor for the fact Melvin doesn't like to be touched. He doesn't want germs on him. He wants to protect himself from other people and especially from relationships.

What does it mean when someone is habitually late? Your friend might arrive late for the party and apologize, mentioning there was an accident and a lot of traffic on the 110. You then hear on the television there was an accident on the freeway. You know your friend is almost always on time. The text tells you what's going on and you believe your friend. But sometimes being late has subtext. In *Sideways*, Miles wakes up late and gets a late start to pick up his friend Jack for their trip to the wine country. We see Miles moving right along on the freeway — no traffic jams, which can be a rarity in California. When he arrives at Jack's home, he tells him he was late because of all the traffic. But we know there wasn't any. Here we're getting into subtext. Why would Mile say that? Several reasons: He's not a totally honest fellow. Later that day, he steals money from his mother, thereby reinforcing the character trait we've seen in his lie to Jack. He doesn't want to admit his life is a bit of a mess, and that oversleeping and drinking too much show something about his deeper problems. And he doesn't like to be blamed.

The subtext for late behavior varies. Maybe the person is young, but doesn't want to admit he doesn't know how to read a clock. Maybe tardiness means the person wants to be the center of attention and make an entrance. Maybe it means the person doesn't care about anybody else's sense of time or schedule and he'll get there whenever he wants. Maybe it's cultural, and the person comes from a culture that doesn't live by the clock, and if someone is late, she doesn't notice, or she expects it. Maybe it's a real psychological problem, showing the person can't get organized. I knew a person once who simply couldn't get anywhere on time. She told me she had been early once, and it made her so nervous she had to drive around the block a number of times to make sure she was late. She was unable to hold down a job and had unrealistic expectations of men, sometimes making statements like: "I'm determined to get married, hopefully within the next two months. I just haven't met the right guy yet! But I'm getting married!" I had no idea what any of it meant, but I knew there was subtext.

Some people make a habit of drumming their fingers on the table, which might show impatience, or that the person is a drummer and is practicing a beat. Or someone might have a habit of clenching his teeth during sleep (as the father did in *Dead Poets Society*), which can indicate that the person is not as calm and in control as he seems to be. In *Dead Poets Society*, this habit also shows how upset the father is about the altercation with his son. It doesn't even shut off when he sleeps.

Shane (from the 1953 film *Shane*) always sits with his back to the wall. What does that mean? He wants to see the door in case a gunslinger unexpectedly comes into the room. Making a point of this ritual (he sits in Joe's chair) strengthens the subtext.

In *Public Enemies* (2009), John Dillinger comes into the hotel room, takes out his gun, opens the window, and closes the curtain. Why? To protect himself. To make sure he hears anyone coming before they come; to make sure they can't see inside. It's his way of making sure there are no surprises.

Some people wear lucky charms, or lucky socks, or a lucky hat. This article might be as simple as a shamrock necklace one friend gives another "for luck," which the friend chuckles and then puts on. But this gesture might contain subtext as well. Often there's a backstory to the charm — it was given by the person's father, now dead. The subtext might be implied if the character says, "I remember my father every time I put this on." Something is underneath the surface of the simple lines. Wearing the charm might also mean the woman doesn't believe she can do it by herself — but needs some "extras" to get her through.

Most of our habitual behaviors have a backstory. The backstory and, therefore, the actions will be different if the person was the favored son or the black sheep of the family. Finding out what went on in the person's family, or other relationships, usually begins to reveal the subtext. But it's not necessary to write the backstory in order for us to understand the subtext. It is often implied by the behavior. We know it's there and can guess what it might be about. In *To Have and Have Not*, a man slaps the face of Slim (Lauren Bacall). Steve (Humphrey Bogart) interprets the subtext because he notices her response to the slap. He understands a crucial part of her backstory and discerns that it included some beatings. Why? Because she didn't blink.

LOOK AT DECISIONS AND CHOICES

What do people decide to do and what do those decisions mean? We can often understand what is really going on by the choices that characters make — either main characters or supporting characters. In *Up in the Air*, Ryan (George Clooney) decides to go to the wedding of his niece, whom he clearly has not seen for some time. It seems to be a new choice for him, because the sister mentions he has not been around the family much over the years. The family is happy and surprised to see him at the wedding. Ryan even offers to walk his niece down the aisle. But the choice has already been made — her fiancé's uncle has already been chosen to do these honors instead of the father (who is absent) or Ryan, the next logical person. Ryan's momentary and subtle crestfallen look tells us he understands his place (or lack of place) in the family, and so do we in the audience.

In *The English Patient* (1996), the Count (Ralph Fiennes) and Katharine (Kristin Scott Thomas) show interest in each other, which marks the beginning of their affair. During the sandstorm, the Count reaches out and touches her hair for the first time. His voice catches for a moment — something has happened between them. Their decision to follow up on this moment begins their affair.

In the third Indiana Jones film, Indiana (Harrison Ford) decides to step out onto the invisible plank to go for the Holy Grail, taking the necessary leap of faith to achieve the goal.

All of these gestures, preceded by a choice, tell us what's going on beneath the surface and often serve as important pivots in a character's transformation.

WHAT IS THE SUBTEXT OBJECTIVE?

Every great story has a goal, which is in the text of the script. The detective wants to capture the criminal and solve the case. The pianist wants to win the piano contest. The secretary wants to move up the corporate ladder. The guy wants to get the girl. The goal is set in Act One and achieved at the end of Act Three. It's clear. It's said in the text. And there may be little or nothing under the surface.

But films rich in subtext have hidden goals under the surface. Much like a lake or river, a script might seem smooth as glass on the surface, but have swift and dangerous currents underneath. The undercurrents reveal themselves throughout the film. What is underneath will eventually trouble the smooth waters.

A writer shades in subtext throughout the script. The actor interprets it. Actors, like the writer and the audience, have to figure out "what's really going on," and play out the subtextual meanings. In acting (particularly Method Acting), the actor figures out both the underlying objective of the scene and the overall objective, called the Super-Objective, for the entire script. The actor then expresses this objective in a phrase that contains a verb: "I want to make him suffer." "I want to tear him apart." "I want to snag him for my husband." "I want to stomp him out of existence." These objectives might guide the actor, even if the text doesn't talk about them. An actor might be determined to "snag a husband," even though the text might show a man and a woman at the no-host bar, discussing whether the red or white wine is better, or the text might be about a woman getting a man's help to change her tire. If she decides (and finds evidence in the script) that the character's main goal is to snag a husband, the actor will continue to play out that goal, signaling the subtext beneath the lines rather than simply speaking the lines at face value.

In an underdog triumph movie, the protagonist has the goal of the text: to win the championship or the competition. But the subtext-objective might be to "prove to Daddy I can do it!" Now there's subtext, because the championship is no longer only about winning the game, but also about resolving a father-son relationship. Or, perhaps the protagonist has an injury and cannot play in the game because of his rehabilitation. Perhaps the coach and the other team players believe he is no longer capable of doing well, or of playing at all. Now the protagonist's objective is not just to play well, but also to prove he's up to the task. Not only is the game at stake, but also his career in sports, his membership on the team, and his reputation. This objective, which exists on the subtextual level, helps drive the actor's emotions and actions for the entire scene. This super-objective unifies the actor's performance and strengthens it for the entire script. The stronger the verb used to express the objective, the stronger the performance.

The actor can't bring subtext to the role if the writer hasn't shaded in any subtext. But sometimes the writer is unaware of the subtext. Some writers intuit what ideas and words best fit in the script, even though they can't tell you exactly what the subtext is. Actors hope there's more to the script than just the text. And the more conscious the writer, the greater the possibility that the script will be unified by a clear objective, even if it lies under the surface.

Although it comes from acting, the concept of the objective and super-objective can be applied to writing and directing as well.

One of the most memorable essays I've read on this subject comes from a director in the 1950s named Harold Clurman. He directed the theatrical production of *Member of the Wedding* (based on a Carson McCullers novel by the same name), which featured Julie Harris as a young girl in her first starring role. Julie plays a twelve-year-old tomboy named Frankie, who is feeling the push and pull of finding her identity. She's trying to figure out where she fits in and she struggles for a sense of belonging. Frankie is going to be in her brother's wedding and decides she wants to go further than this — she wants to go with him on his honeymoon as well. Her desire causes a lot of angst for everyone in the family.

Clurman chose as the super-objective for the film: "to get connected." Choosing the super-objective for the character, Clurman found evidence of the idea within the script and phrased it in a way that was helpful to him as the director and to the actor. He saw each character seeking the same objective, but each approached the action differently. Clurman then found certain stage directions within the text that reinforced this idea and added more: "Frankie scrapes her head against door." It's as if Frankie is trying to connect with everything, animate and inanimate objects alike. He analyzes how her desire for connection works: "Frankie is hostile. You hate what you can't connect with and want to hurt it. Or you want to hurt yourself for failing to make the connection." He sees that the little boy in the play, John Henry, wants to "learn to connect." Frankie's father wants "to stay in touch." Jarvis, the brother who's getting married, wants "to make the simplest connection, with... a nice girl." Another character wants "to make as much connection as he can find" and another, "to force connection (or die)." By clarifying this objective, Clurman integrated the production. (footnote: From "Some Preliminary Notes for The Member of the Wedding" by Harold Clurman, from *Directors on Directing: A Source Book of the Modern Theater*, edited by Toby Cole & Helen Krich Chinoy. Macmillan Publishing, N.Y., 1963.p. 380-389.)

Gestures that imply the subtext can be added by the writer (sometimes put into the stage directions), the director, or the actor. It's not unusual for actors to ignore the stage directions, and come up with their own, or to follow the stage directions almost exactly because they seem appropriate and helpful for the role. For writers, this super-objective could also be called the subtext-objective. It's the driving force of the story. It's the underlying action that, like an undercurrent, runs beneath the surface. It's a strong action with direction. The stronger the flow, the greater the desire to achieve this objective, and the more tension, conflict, and subtext there is. By having a sub-text-objective, as well as a text objective, the underlying current adds depth and direction.

This subtext-objective can work in three ways:

1. All the characters in a script can be working toward the same super-objective, as in the *Member of the Wedding* example. They all want the same thing, but are working toward it in different ways. Some of those ways can be effective, some harmful. Their different methods, which can clash with each other, cause tension and conflict.

2. A major character, or other characters, might be working toward the super-objective, but other major or supporting characters may not be on board. Sometimes they transform during the course of the story until most (but usually not the antagonist) are moving in the same direction.

3. The protagonist and antagonist have opposing super-objectives; they clearly want the flow to go in opposite directions.

BREAKING DOWN THE SUBTEXT-OBJECTIVE

1. *Ordinary People* is a very rich subtextual film, in which everyone has the same general super-objective, but they work it out in different ways.

In the story, Beth and Calvin had two sons — Bucky, the older one (and the mother's favorite), and Conrad. In the backstory, the boys were involved in a boating accident. Bucky drowned and Conrad lived. Mother, father, and son struggle with sorrow, guilt, and regret. Conrad attempts suicide. The film begins after he returns from the mental hospital, where he's spent some months.

The subtext-objective of the story and the characters could be defined as: "to return to normal." All the characters seem, in one way or another, to relate to the idea of normal — to a greater or lesser degree.

Beth, the mother, is desperate to return to her normal life. She doesn't want to talk about the accident or about Bucky or the mental hospital. When Conrad doesn't eat his French toast because he's not hungry, and then mentions the hospital, she quickly clears the table and throws the French toast into the garbage disposal — thus, in essence, throwing out the discussion and, subtextually, throwing out the disturbing event, which was partly caused by Conrad.

She tries to return to normal by making everything perfect. Her table napkins are perfectly folded. The Halloween treats for trick-or-treaters are a work of art. She says, "It's time we got back to normal." When Conrad tries to help her and talk to her, she tells him to go up and clean out his messy closet, to make it neat and normal and not to have such mess in their lives. She says "I don't want any more change in my life." She doesn't want to deal with any emotions.

She tries to return to normal by doing normal activities — setting the table neatly, playing golf, going to dinner parties, and turning away when emotions or the accident are mentioned. She scolds Calvin after a cocktail party for telling another guest that Conrad is going to a psychiatrist. That's private, according to Beth. She suggests to Calvin that they go to Houston to visit her brother and his wife during the holidays, leaving Conrad with the grandmother. During their visit, they laugh, drink cocktails, play golf, and act as if nothing has happened to mar their lives.

Conrad tries to return to normal — singing in the choir, con-
tinuing to compete on the swimming team, going to school,
coming to dinner — but it doesn't work. He finally agrees to go
to a psychiatrist, who doesn't set much store on normal. Dr.
Berger helps Conrad find a new life, without the same limits
that demand no emotion and not talking about things. Dr.
Berger believes in the reality of life, in confronting problems,
looking at them and feeling them. What comes out of that may
not be normal at all, but it's life and it's truth.

For his part, Calvin is caught trying to live the normal life his
wife demands, but his love, and feelings for his living son prevent him from denying there is something wrong. Normal,
for him, has become a cover-up. He becomes willing to look
at the truth, about what normal in their lives has been. He realizes Beth doesn't love Conrad, that Beth is not a giver, that
Beth can't face certain things. And he realizes that he probably
doesn't love her anymore. As a result, Beth quickly packs and
leaves. Calvin admits about there are serious problems in his
marriage.

                    CALVIN
        It would have been all right if there
              hadn't been a mess.

Other supporting and even minor characters relate to normal in different ways. Calvin's business buddies talk incessantly
about business, whether at cocktail parties or while jogging. As
long as they're on the treadmill of business, everything is
normal and must be alright.

Some of Beth's friends go about their normal activities asking
no questions about Conrad; others do, and Beth replies that all
is fine, although she's deeply embarrassed when she discovers
he has quit the swimming team and not even told her. Decep-
tion is not normal. Embarrassing Beth in front of her friend is
not normal. Quitting the swimming team is not what their son
should be doing.

Conrad's friend Karen, whom he met in the mental hospital, tries to convince him, and herself, that all is fine, all is normal – and then she kills herself.

Conrad's new friend, Jeanine, is real and hasn't yet found her normal. She's trying to find her way and she's willing to admit the truth when she doesn't handle something well, when she's embarrassed, when she isn't sure how to act. For her, being natural is important. And it's normal for her to be natural.

Although a few lines here and there clearly show various responses to normal, most of this current moves in the subtext. Everyone is struggling with what is normal. Even the context of the story shows what would be considered the normal middle and upper class world – and how that world can be marred and destroyed by an accident.

This subtext-objective helps actors, director, editor, and even the art department and composer, all move in the same direction. The writer maps out the underlying current, the actor searches for the inherent meanings and the emotions of the story, and everyone else, hopefully, gets on board so they are all working together toward the same meaning for the good of the film.

Sometimes it takes a while for the writer to figure out the underlying meanings. The subtext might be unconscious to the writer for several drafts of the script. Sometimes, the super-objective an actor chooses may not be what the writer expressed. Even when the writer is able to clarify the subtext, care must be taken not to put it into the text for the sake of convenience. Subtext sometimes seeps into the text, leading to on-the-nose dialogue and action. The subtext disappears, and everything is now simply in the text.

2. Sometimes there's a subtext-objective that relates to most of the characters, but it might take some time for other characters to get on board. In the film *The Fugitive*, we clearly know the

objective of most characters because it's found in the text: Richard Kimble wants to be proven innocent; Sam Gerard wants to capture him and do his job; Charlie Nichols and the One-Armed Man want to make sure they aren't found out. It's all straightforward. Although the film does not have a great deal of subtext, an implication of subtext could have been played further. There is a suggestion within the story that Richard wants more than just to be found innocent — he wants justice, which means to make things right again. In one of his lines, he says, "everything ... was taken from me." Justice would mean resolution. But he also realizes there was a motivation for his wife's murder, which was related to a cover-up about a medicine that had just gone on the market. Dr. Nichols has manipulated the facts. Kimble wants to resolve this conspiracy as well.

An earlier draft of the script has a scene in which Richard goes back to the condo where he lived with Helen. The condo is now owned by someone else and the new owners are having a party. Richard stands across the street looking into the home. The scene implies yearning, what was and is no longer, a sense of loss and the desire to return to what he had. Justice means making things right again. Some of his later actions show him trying to make things right by discovering the truth about the medicine. Creating a subtext-objective allows the writer to deepen the action and play to other layers of meaning.

Whereas Richard wants justice, Sam Gerard doesn't care much about justice. He simply wants to find Richard. But, as the film proceeds, he becomes interested in justice and moves from "I don't care," to knowing Richard is innocent, and becoming determined to get the bad guy, not just to do the job.

Sam Gerard is not moving in the same direction as Richard until the third act. The issue of justice then plays out, not just with Kimble, but also with Gerard's recognition that the One-Armed Man is "dirty," and that the corporation Devlin-McGregor is a "monster." He and Richard, by Act

101

Three, are swimming in the same direction, although the antagonists (Charlie and the One-Armed Man) are still swimming in the opposite direction.

In *New in Town* (2009), Lucy's objective seems to be the same as that of the owners of the plant: to close it down. This objective is counter to the objective of the people of the town. As the story proceeds, Lucy changes direction and joins the people of the town to save their plant. She was moving with one current but, by the end, is moving with another.

Remains of the Day has an undercurrent of characters wanting "to get closer." Miss Kenton wants to get close to Mr. Stevens. She goads him, has evening discussions with him, and tries to get a rise out of him. In his undercurrent, he wants the same thing, but keeps pulling back. He's not able to go with the flow. A few times he reaches out, tentatively, but then pulls back. He lives by decorum, which is destructive to his emotional life.

Other characters, such as Lord Darlington, the owner of the mansion, wants to get close to the Nazis, and they want to get close to him. Stevens Sr. wants to get close to his work, and get close to his son, but the son resists and Stevens Sr. is demoted to a lesser job.

3. In most films, the text and the subtext-objective of the protagonist opposes the text and subtext-objective of the antagonist. One starts flowing with the direction of the current, or starts by setting the direction of the current, and the other resists and wants to turn things in a different direction. If the current is flowing downstream, one wants to switch it upstream. If the story is swimming upstream, a character wants it to move downstream. The countercurrent provides tension and conflict.

In most crime dramas, most action-adventures, and many romantic stories, we see resistance and counter-resistance. Although they will always be in the text, occasionally they are also in the subtext.

In *Avatar* Jake's and the Colonel's objective seem to be the same: to find a diplomatic solution to gaining the nonobtanium from the Na'vis. But in the subtext, the Colonel wants to blow them away and Jake wants the opposite – to become one of them. His subtext-objective is implied the first time he becomes an Avatar and experiences being able to run again. As the story goes on, Jake's true objective becomes clearer, as does the Colonel's. Clearly they are at crosscurrents with each other.

Understanding the various currents of a story and of characters can help you create a point and counterpoint – the contrast between the surface of the story and its undercurrents. This insight can help you show character transformations, as a character switches from one current to another, often eventually moving in the opposite direction. Although they will always be in the text, resistance and counter-resistance are occasionally also in the subtext.

103

EXERCISES AND QUESTIONS FOR DISCUSSION

(1) Watch *Ordinary People* and see how many specific instances you can find when the subtext regarding "getting back to normal" is implied, but not talked about. How many times is this notion expressed through gestures rather than through words?

(2) Choose a film you believe is rich in subtext. How would you define the subtext-objective? What are the currents you see flowing underneath the surface? Do they flow in the same general direction or are they crosscurrents?

(3) Look at your script. Are there times when you've talked about a subject, but could show it through gestures or actions without any words at all?

(4) Read a script and look at the stage directions. Are there places you would change them to imply more subtext? Can you think of other gestures an actor could do that would make the film and the performances even better?

(5) You may want to read the Harold Clurman essay from *Directors on Directing* (you can get second-hand copies of the book) or other essays about the actor's objective and super-objective. Then apply what you learned about the actor's work to your work and analysis as a writer.

CHAPTER FIVE
CHAPTER FIVE

creating subtext through images and metaphors

Film implies meaning through images, not just through words, gestures, and action. We see a visual image that, if it contains subtext, will carry unconscious associations. The visual will then mean more than just what we see — it will imply a whole range of other meanings and emotions. We understand the subtext because one image and one idea, well expressed, imply all sorts of hidden meanings.

In the famous eating scene of *Tom Jones* (1963), as Tom and the voluptuous Tart eat dinner and dig into their turkey thigh, we know their lust for their food is really their lust for each other. In *The Piano* (1993), when Baines dusts the piano, we know he's not merely dusting the piano, but also thinking about stroking Ada. These images and actions tell us what's really going on.

LOOK TO SEASON, WEATHER SYSTEMS, AND TIME OF DAY

It might truly be a dark and stormy night, but in most cases, this image will imply other meanings. In our youth, a dark and stormy night probably created some trepidation. Stormy nights were scary, and we still remember them. The writer simply has to evoke the associations many of us bring to an image, and capitalize on it to create subtext.

When we see the stormy night, we might suspect danger is near. The writer uses the weather to imply things brewing beneath the surface. If the writer wanted to tell us there wasn't any danger, the scene may have been set on a calm and clear night. Or, if the writer wanted to suggest something magical and wonderful was about to happen, perhaps there'd be a falling star and the moon would be casting its light on a path with a child or some charming elf-like creature merrily skipping along.

When Shakespeare wanted to show there was a storm raging in a character's heart, he added weather to his plays. "Blow, winds, and crack your cheeks! Rage! Blow!" says King Lear, as his own rage echoes the stormy night. It rains in the film *Doubt* (by John Patrick Shanley), as the tension between Father Flynn and Sister Aloysius builds. In the beginning of *Shutter Island* (2010), as Teddy Daniels (Leonardo di Caprio) arrives at the island, the captain of the boat says "storm coming" – of course, and in more ways than one. In the farce *Airplane!* (1980), as the plane makes its way to Chicago, hoping to land in spite of the sick pilots and passengers, there's a storm. Things are dire! There is lots of thunder and lightening and rain. It doesn't look as if it'll make it! But of course it does!

In *Psycho*, when Mary steals the money and leaves town, the directions say, "There is something vaguely ominous about the darkening sky into which the car seems to be disappearing." The ominous sky implies the storm within Mary as she escapes with the money. The visual metaphor is strengthened in the script by the word "disappearing." Mary will disappear into the darkness of the swamp and it will be difficult to find her. A storm also brews in *A Streetcar Named Desire* (1951) as sexual tension mounts between Stanley Kowalski and Blanche DuBois.

Rain can mean we don't see clearly and are lost in a downpour. Or, it can mean a time of cleansing when everything bad is washed away. Sometimes it implies the tears a character is unable to produce. In *The English Patient* (1996), when the war is over, it rains. The past is washed away. Hana brings the English patient outside to feel the fresh falling rain, which waters and nurtures the earth and washes away the years of war. He is carried around a pond, with laughter and joy. The attitudes of the characters reinforce the subtext of the scene.

The seasons tell us about mood and meaning in a film. During what time of year does your story take place? In spring, as flowers bloom and the birds sing and everything is young and alive like new-found love? In fall, a time of nostalgia for lost love and a time of change? In summer, perhaps, when it's hot and sultry, like the passion that inflames the lovers?

In *Dead Poets Society*, Neil commits suicide in the winter. There's a sound of thunder in the background. It's nighttime. Neil is dead and cold. Snow falls and covers the earth just as the father covered up his involvement in the suicide so he could blame it on Keating. The reader will read the metaphor, the audience will see the metaphor, and both will be pulled further into the story. A connection is created that is visceral, functioning at an unspoken level with the audience.

In *The Godfather: Part II*, after most of Michael's competitors are dead, after his wife has had a miscarriage (really an abortion), and his brother has betrayed him, Michael returns home. It's winter. The children's playthings in the yard are covered with snow — the swings, his son's little car. They're immobile. Still. Michael says, "Times are changing," and they are. But right now, things are still covered up.

At what time of day does your scene take place? At the dawn of a new day, filled with possibilities? In the gritty dark, when acts can be secretive, hidden in the shadows? At high noon? At cocktail hour or the witching hour? Nighttime carries different associations than a bright sunny day.

The writer might choose to create a contrast, such as putting a death in the spring when everything is beginning to bloom. In spite of death, life goes on. The writer might choose to have the death occur during the fall, a time of transition, when life is beginning to wither, nature is changing from full bloom to death. Or perhaps the person dies in summer, when everything is alive and fun and energetic, indicating that the dying person and those around the bedside are missing out on life. In *Dr. Zhivago* (1965), love blooms and reaches fruition in the middle of winter, as the two lovers stay in the cold country.

All details can have meaning, but care must be taken. The writer needs to make sure the details in a script are not arbitrary, as if there is no thought behind how the image fits the idea. Sometimes the choice of images can be cliché — as when lovers walk on the beach at sunset or flowers bloom as they have their first kiss. Images have meaning and writers think through the meanings to make sure they're fresh and clear.

CREATING CONTEXT

The writer creates the context of the story through visuals. Where does it take place? What kind of a place is it? What associations does the writer want us to bring as we watch this world?

Does the first scene take place in wide open spaces, in a home, office, theater, or a country estate? Are these spaces large, or small and claustrophobic? What does that quality say about the story and the psychology of the characters?

If the writer sets the location in a bar, what kind of bar is it? And what does the writer's choice mean? What is being communicated to the audience? There's a famous scene in *The Graduate* (1967) when Benjamin takes Elaine to a strip club. Elaine is enthusiastic about the date, until the entertainment begins. She becomes embarrassed and humiliated. Why did Benjamin take her to this kind of bar? Because he's sleeping with Elaine's mother and he resents being forced to go out on this date.

In Hitchcock's *Shadow of a Doubt*, Uncle Charlie takes his niece to a "smoky and hot" bar. Why? The location suggests a variety of possible subtexts, but when we watch the scene, or read the script, some subtexts are suggested, others are not. On the surface Uncle Charlie seems respectable, yet he takes her to a disreputable place. We might wonder if Uncle Charlie is truly disgusting and wants to make a pass at her. But there's nothing in the script or film that suggests this likelihood. We might wonder if he takes her to that bar to show her she isn't as sophisticated as she might think she is. He wants her to know she doesn't know the ways of the world. He's worried she's guessing that he really is a murderer and he wants her to know that if that is indeed what she thinks, she doesn't know what she's talking about because she lacks sophistication. Evidence in the scene indicates that this last suggestion is, in fact, one of his motivations. He talks to her as if she were a child.

> UNCLE CHARLIE
> You think you know something... ? You think you're the
> clever little girl who knows something.
> But there's so much you don't know.

His use of the words "little girl" and "so much you don't know" conveys his attitude. But then he tries another tack, one that implies she is sophisticated enough to know the ways of the world, and that people make mistakes, and she should know to leave well enough alone.

> UNCLE CHARLIE
> ... And if you've heard some little
> things about me, why I guess you're
> enough of a woman of the world to
> overlook them.

Uncle Charlie switches subtexts, trying to get at his niece in any way possible, to make sure she doesn't guess and, above all, doesn't tell, the truth about him. The smoky bar gives him the upper hand, because it's a dark and grown-up place — in a sense, what Uncle Charlie is asking Young Charlie to be.

Both *The Messenger* and *The Hurt Locker* have scenes in a grocery store. A grocery store can represent the mundane, normal, everyday world. The war is anything but that. In *The Hurt Locker* (2008), the grocery store motivates the character to return to the war, where lives are at stake (including his), and where there's a clearly defined job and he knows what he needs to do.

In *Silence of the Lambs* (1991, by Ted Tally from the novel by Thomas Harris), the prison cell tells us much about Hannibal Lecter. The description tells us about its "sparse, bolted down furniture, many soft cover books and papers. On the walls, extraordinarily detailed, skillful drawings, mostly European cityscapes in charcoal or crayon."

Notice how this detail about the books and drawings begins to tell us that Lecter wants to be somewhere else — to get out. It also indicates he's well-traveled and cultured. He has an artistic side. This complexity makes the horror of what he does even more grisly.

When Clarice enters, he turns to her and "considers her." His power of observation is clearly very keen. The description draws our focus onto Hannibal's "glittering eyes, and the wet red mouth," which gives us a sense of his deviance. He is a blood-eater. And he's eager. He's described as the "gracious host." His voice is "cultured and soft," but we soon learn he's a monster who hides behind well-mannered ways.

Sometimes the context is laden with subtext and we suspect there is something going on but we're meant to experience the mystery before the subtext becomes clear. This strategy works well, especially if we are not merely confused. The beginning of *Inglourious Basterds* (2009) opens on a bucolic French dairy farm. Then we see cars in the distance coming closer. A Nazi officer and his soldiers arrive. There is a sense of threat, in spite of the politeness between the farmer and his daughters, and the German officer. The subtext is thick with meaning. There's a heaviness, a secrecy, a reticence. We ask ourselves, "What's going on? Something is happening here. There's some secret!" Then, we realize what the subtext is: There are Jews hiding beneath the floorboards. Now the subtext has become text, as the film shows us the Jews and we understand the situation.

CREATING THE STRONG VISUAL IMAGE

Sometimes visual metaphors run throughout the entire film, reminding us over and over again what the film is really about. Movies such as *Chocolat* (2000), *Like Water for Chocolate* (1992), or *Babette's Feast* (1987) are not just about food, but are also really about love and life and what's important. Even the feast that the Spirit of Christmas Present shows Scrooge in *The Christmas Carol* is a metaphor for the way Scrooge does not partake in the richness of life.

Sometimes the visual metaphor simply tells us what is going on. *All Quiet on the Western Front* (1930) features a famous image of a flower that gets crushed in the mud. And that's what happens in war – good things get crushed. In films where houses are built, or torn down, the house often serves as a metaphor for the growth, or decline, of a character. In *Life as a House* (2001), the building of the house epitomizes George Monroe's (Kevin Kline) decline as a result of his terminal illness, but also shows his spiritual growth.

Sometimes the context is the period in which the story takes place. In *The White Ribbon* (2010), which takes place in prewar Europe, the bicycle represents the encroaching modern world.

In *Modern Times* (1936), the clock gives a sense of time passing and change occurring. *The Last Picture Show* (1971) uses the image of the last picture show to represent change coming to a small town. In *The Gladiator* (2000) Maximus (Russell Crowe) strokes the wheat fields as he walks. The sound of children laughing in the background represents his home, which he misses and is on a quest to return to.

In *Jacob's Ladder* (1990), when Jacob (Tim Robbins) accepts his own death, he's led up the stairs by his young son who died a few years earlier. Walking up into the light on a staircase symbolizes the rising of the soul into the light of God. It is also reminiscent of Jacob's Ladder in the Bible, which climbs up to God. Some of us might even have a slight association with Jack and the Beanstalk, which features a type of ladder that also leads to riches.

Our associations with many different objects and visual features come from our real life experiences, as well as from a collective unconscious. Through the years, objects and visuals accrue meaning for us. Writers can draw on those meanings to awaken these associations within the audience.

SOUND METAPHORS

Some films become well known for their sound metaphors. True, a train whistle might simply announce a train is coming, but in a certain context, a train whistle can carry a sense of loneliness, of long journeys, or having no money so one has to ride the rails. Listen to the train whistles in *3:10 to Yuma* (1957 and 2007) or in *High Noon* (1952), where it announces threat and trepidation, or in *Bound for Glory* (1976) (the story of Woody Guthrie), and see if the train whistle carries other meanings about his journey, about poverty, about hopelessness, or about loneliness.

In one of the first scenes in *Jaws* (1975), Chrissy, the girl who will be attacked by a shark within minutes of the opening of the movie, goes swimming. As she swims out from the shore, the nearby buoy dings its bell. On one level, it's simply a buoy bell, but it also has the sound of a death knell. It helps add tension to the scene and foreshadows what will soon happen to Chrissy.

At the beginning of *Shutter Island*, as the boat lands on the island, the musical score features three blasts, sounding like a foghorn and yet warning of danger. Foghorns usually sound when people are lost and can't see in the fog, an apt metaphor for the problems the characters face in the film.

In *Valkryrie*, Stauffenberg plays the record "The Ride of the Valkyries," Richard Wagner's s great German musical work of triumph, victory, and conquering. Yet, it's played during a bombing, which is a contrast to the victorious crescendo of the music. Obviously victory isn't quite so easy, as evidenced by the falling plaster as the music builds.

This same music is used in *Apocalypse Now* (1979, written by Michael Herr, based on the novella *Heart of Darkness* by Joseph Conrad), as the men surf while napalm is dropped nearby. The men believe they're dwelling in god-like safety, but they're not.

The movie *On the Waterfront* (1954) plays with the cooing of pigeons. Devorah Cutler-Rubenstein, in her book *What's the Big Idea: Writing Shorts*, discusses the use of the pigeons in this film and how they tell us about the subtext. She explains:

> Terry Malloy (Marlon Brando) raises pigeons and he's a stool pigeon. Throughout the film, the pigeons echo the story and his character. Their flapping of wings represent the freedom he would like to have which is also carried by the sounds of the seagulls on the water front, as they dive and coo. The pigeons are friendly and chirpy when he's talking to his love. The sounds are frenetic when he's confronting the bad guys. Malloy is a scavenger, tied to the droppings left to him by others. He is trapped in his relationship to the mob, waiting for the next handout, just like his pet pigeons.

114   Sometimes the music score gives us clues about the subtext, cuing how we're supposed to react to the movie. In *Bonnie and Clyde*, the music is happy-go-lucky when they do their first robberies, indicating it's just a merry romp and nobody is really getting hurt. As the robberies continue, there is less music; by the end, the music becomes quite somber.

In *The Messenger*, we hear the music to "Home on the Range" three times. First, an ice cream truck plays it, and we hear it in the distance as the men have just notified the Next of Kin about the death of their loved one. The music sits in stark contrast to the tragedy and grief of the preceding scene. Next time, the two men sing it in the car, and we know that not all is happy nor do these men really have homes. The third time it's played over the end credits. "Home on the Range" is about a contented place "where the skies are not cloudy all day." The skies in this film are cloudy, and it's unclear what home really is for these men.

As you work with sound in your scripts, think about simple sounds that can add layers to the story, either working to add another level to the scene (the buoy of *Jaws*) or contradicting the themes ("Home on the Range") to deepen the meaning through counterpoint.

CREATING METAPHORS THROUGH PROPS

Objects often carry deep associations, as Freud taught us to believe. A knife might be used for the slicing or chopping for which it was designed, but it can also imply a threat, a potential murder weapon, a warning — all depending on how it's handled.

A rope can simply be a prop to tie up the horse and mean nothing more than that obvious usefulness. But a rope can also imply a lynch mob is on its way. It can imply capture and a loss of freedom. It can be a way to keep someone, or some animal, in line and contained. All of these ideas can enrich a

film by telling us about the theme and even creating emotions
of fear, concern, or empathy.

Both the film *The Cider House Rules* (1999) and Hitchcock's *Psycho* have lists of rules that in turn tell us something about whether the characters live by them or not. *Psycho*'s opening scene in the hotel room features a list of rules on the mirror. Yet, this story is about a great many rules that will be broken.

Mirrors often have meaning as reflections of our own lives or windows into other realities. In *Psycho*, a mirror rests over the bureau, yet when Mary puts on her earrings, the directions say, Mary is "not bothering or perhaps not wanting to look at herself in the mirror." In this case, the shabby room stands for Mary's shabby life. The avoidance of the mirror reinforces the sleaziness of the affair and her desire for some respectability.

Mirrors can also indicate that two people are opposites; or, two people might be similar, and one might be a reflection of the other. Mirrors might show an image of someone trapped within an identity. In *Watcher in the Woods* (1980), the mirror is the link to the girl who disappeared from that area many years ago.

Face-Off (1997) plays with the theme of identity, using broken mirrors to visually shatter the body image and reduce the hunter and hunted to a game of survival for both.

Birds that are alive can carry subtexts about freedom and soaring. In *Dead Poets Society*, a large flock of birds in a meadow excitedly flies up in the air, and then the film cuts to the next scene, showing the excited boys on their first day of school, moving together, like a flock, toward their classes.

Birds that are dead carry an entirely different subtext. In *Psycho*, Mary enters Norman's parlor and is startled to see a room full of stuffed birds. Of course, this image later clarifies why Norman was able to keep his mother "stuffed" for some years, but it also creates a weird context of dead things and shows us a person who tries to keep things alive, even after they've died. Also in the room are paintings of nudes that contain some religious overtones. Weird. Disturbing. Fascinating.

There is also the resonance of "birds" in Mary's last name, Crane. Mary won't get stuffed, but she does fly away with the money (metaphorically speaking), and she will soon be dead just like the birds she sees.

Props such as furniture can tell us about the real meanings of a story. The size of a desk and the placement of desks in an office tell us about each person's importance, or lack of it. The bigger the desk, the more removed it is from others, and the fewer the papers on the desk, the higher the status. If the desk is in a private office, all the better. If the office has a window, better yet, and if the office is at a corner with a view, clearly that person is very important. In *Mad Men* (2007-present) it's clear to someone breaking in, especially to the old boy's club, that the desk and office are very important. In *Working Girl* (1998), moving from a cubicle to an office with a window is a huge victory. I suspect all of us who have been secretaries in a cubicle could celebrate with Tess over that move!

Cars can also carry subtext, telling us who is rich and powerful, who is important, or if someone is counter-culture. Some years ago I discovered that my status had gone up because someone saw me in my little red sports car. It became clear through a few well-timed questions that he thought I would drive a car like a gray Honda — clearly not a status symbol in Hollywood. I laughed and said I used to drive a gray Honda, but my favorite color is red and I discovered that red cars don't cost anymore than gray ones. But I also was greatly amused that I had achieved some type of status in Hollywood.

In some films, jewelry represents power, sometimes even being a symbol of power and control. In *Titanic* (1997), Rose casts the emerald back into the sea because her treasure was her love and her life, not just an object.

Photographs are good props and carry many associations. *Fatal Attraction* ends with a photograph of the happy family, together, and it does seem that things are now fine, since Alex has been killed. But the photograph adds a bit of a question at the end: Will all be all right now, or not?

In *Back to the Future* (1985), the photograph of Marty begins disappearing, just as his existence will disappear if he doesn't return to the present. It shows time is running out.

In *Sideways*, right before Miles steals money from his mother, he sees a photograph of himself and his ex-wife on their wedding day — clearly in happier times. The photograph, on the textual level, shows us Miles was married. On the subtextual level, it deepens his character by showing a contrast, how his life is now going sideways, rather than straight ahead. Not until the end of the film do we begin to see Miles moving in a forward direction.

In *Ordinary People*, Calvin would like to get a photo of Beth and Conrad, but it's clear Beth doesn't want closeness to Conrad, in a picture, or otherwise. The scene begins with the grandmother trying to take a photo, but she isn't sure how to aim the camera. She can't quite see Conrad in the photo and asks, "Where are you?" which is a good question, considering that neither Conrad nor Beth know where they are in the scheme of things at this point in the story. They are still finding their way. The grandfather tells Conrad to get in the middle between his mother and father, a place where Conrad really doesn't want to be. The grandfather tells his wife to "hold it level" (which is difficult to do in this family — since they aren't on the level and they certainly aren't in focus). Calvin then decides he wants a photo of Conrad and Beth. Beth suggests instead:

118

> BETH
> No, I tell you what. Let's get...
> three men in there, and I'll take a
> picture of you.

> CALVIN
> Connie, move in a little closer to
> your mother. Okay... prize
> winner...

Calvin clicks but it doesn't work.... Just as there are a great many things in this family that don't work.

Beth hopes to get out of it.

> BETH
> Calvin...

> CALVIN
> Hold it. Connie, smile!

> BETH
> Calvin!

> CALVIN
> Just a second, smile!

> BETH
> Calvin, give me the camera.
> CALVIN

> No, I didn't get it yet...

> BETH
> Come on, give me the camera.

> CONRAD
> Dad, give her the camera.

> CALVIN
> I want a really good picture of the
> two of you. OK?

                   BETH
    No, but I really want a shot of the
      three of you men. Give me the
        camera, Calvin. Please...

                  CALVIN
    Not until I get a picture of the
            two of you.

                  BETH
                  Cal?

               CONRAD
              (shouts)
    GIVE-HER-THE-GODDAMN-CAMERA!

Finally, Beth takes the camera and takes a photo of Calvin. And
then quickly changes the subject.

                  BETH
     Who's hungry? I'll make the
           sandwiches.

Once again, Beth avoids the problem facing all of them.

A photo freezes a moment — usually a happy moment. But this
film is about a family in flux. The photo remains elusive.

Veils and curtains can have meaning. In *Inglourious Basterds*, before
Emmanuelle starts her plan to kill the Nazis in her cinema, she
pulls down the lace veil on her hat. The subterfuge is ready to
begin. The plan has been covered up, and will remain covered
until it's put into action.

The Last Emperor (1987) has many images of curtains, dividing the
common people from the Imperial Emperor and his people.

A ring is often used in films with strong mythic meanings. The
Ring in *The Lord of the Rings* movies (2001, 2002, 2003) stands
for an ancient dark pact between kings and power. The Ring
takes over Frodo's mind and his choice to do good. But if he

can conquer its power, evil will lose. The Ring also implies the cyclic nature of reality, a symbol of continuity and wholeness, be it of individuals, seasons, or civilizations. Since a ring typically implies a certain status, such as a wedding ring, or a papal or royal ring, receiving one, putting it on, taking it off, or throwing it away can carry subtext about a character's acceptance or rejection of that social status or social role.

A web can be a strong metaphor, as in the *Spiderman* series of films. In *Spiderman 2*, Mary Jane is tied up in the center of a large web. Spiderman crawls toward her, across the web, much as a male spider creates his own courtship ritual, moving across the web to his hoped-for mate.

Keys are often used to signify entrance into a new type of life. They can mean initiation, or opening the door to knowledge, or movement through a door or into a chamber that holds mysteries and possibilities. In *Will Success Spoil Rock Hunter?* (1957) an ad executive vies for the gold bathroom key, which signifies a step up the corporate ladder and, supposedly, into a better life. But he realizes how hollow it is when he achieves it. The first *Batman* movie features a symbolic handing over of the keys to the city and in *The Apartment* (1960) there is the handing over of keys to the apartment.

Just as the drawings and books in *Silence of the Lambs* give us a sense that Lector wants to "get out," the book Mr. Stevens reads in *Remains of the Day* tells us a world about what's going on beneath this rigid and distinguished exterior. It helps us understand that Mr. Stevens thinks of the possibilities of romance – he just doesn't know what to do about it.

Miss Kenton comes to his room with a vase of flowers. She notices he's reading, and first wonders if he has enough light to read. Then she gets curious about what he's reading. He doesn't want to show her and shuts the book, stands up, and holds it protectively. Miss Kenton becomes more curious and wonders,

"Is it racy?" He backs up and gets cornered, as she moves closer, reaching for the book. She keeps insisting on seeing it, finally taking the book from him. They are close and, as you watch the scene, you see a small reaction from Stevens to her closeness. He almost reaches out his hand to touch her hair, and there is the subtle clenching around the mouth, as he is uncomfortable, and yet desiring a connection. She finally opens the book and is surprised by what he's reading.

```
                 MISS KENTON
      It's just a sentimental old love story.
```

Since Stevens wouldn't want her to think he's interested in romance, he explains why he's reading it.

```
                  STEVENS
     I read these books – any books – to develop
            my command and knowledge of
   the English language. I read to further my education.
```

At this point, we in the audience are undoubtedly thinking, "Yeah. Sure." And Miss Kenton has a similar reaction: "Ah, I see." And, of course, we do see and don't believe a word of it.

At the end of *The Messenger*, Olivia is ready to move. A few boxes outside still need to be moved into the moving van. Will moves almost everything into the van. As Olivia and Will start to say good-bye, she invites him into the house to give him her address. They walk inside. Left halfway between the house and the moving van is the last object to be moved, the piano bench. It is the last image of the film and evokes the sense of the betweenness, a sense of ambiguity, and a feeling that Olivia is not totally moving away, but will remain connected to Will in one way or another.

EXPRESSING SUBTEXT THROUGH CHARACTER METAPHORS

Great characters will sometimes use metaphors in their dialogue, which livens their identity. Sometimes, the language they use is just what we might expect. A sports figure might use sports metaphors, whether or not he's talking about sports. He might say, "It's a winning idea," or "It's a slam dunk," or ask, "Did you score tonight?" A lawyer, teacher, or minister might say "Do it by the book," or perhaps an archer might tell us "It's straight as an arrow." Someone who is very kinesthetic (perhaps a nurse, massage therapist, or furrier) might pat someone's shoulder, or stroke a fur, or rub someone's hands to warm him up. In these cases, this metaphor is in the text, not the subtext, since it lines up with what we already know about the character.

Sometimes the metaphors a character uses belie what we understand about the character and reveal hidden dimensions about him or her. Suppose a character tells us he's a peaceable kind of guy. He says he's a pacifist, would never hurt a fly, doesn't believe in war, and only votes for the Peace Candidate (if there is one!) But the metaphors in his language suggest otherwise. They're filled with references to violence. He says "Sock it to me," and "He's punch drunk." He tells his employees to "Hit me with another idea!" and says "You could have knocked me over with a feather," "We've been attacked by the Right!" and "The guy tripped me up!" If you notice these metaphors, you might suspect things are not as they seem.

You might have a character who's an accountant but who really wants to be a musician. The metaphors he uses tell us about this underlying desire. He might say "I'm not in tune with my girlfriend," or ask someone to "Keep it down to a dull roar!" or say "It's music to my ears."

Or, a person who secretly wants to be an artist might say, "I see," and "I'm blue today," or says "I'm clashing with my boss."

These metaphors can be in the language, but they can also be part of the gestures and action the character demonstrates. The accountant who loves music but doesn't want to admit he really wants to be a musician might hum while he works, or always have the radio playing in the background on a music station. The person who secretly wants to be an artist doodles while talking on the phone.

I began to notice these metaphors more consciously some years ago when interviewing a writer. I noticed his language was peppered with spiritual metaphors. They seemed to lean toward Eastern religions, as he used words like "being mindful" or "detachment," so I was surprised when he said he was Presbyterian. After telling me this information, he paused, and said, "But I'm actually closest to Buddhism." He went on to talk about the difficulty of practicing Buddhism in any communal way because he lived in a small town. He said he wanted to raise his children in the church in order to give them a basis in faith, and mentioned that his grandfather was a minister and saw no reason to rock that boat. But he admitted, "My way of looking at life is really Buddhist!" which his language implied.

Recently, I was working on a script where most of the characters were colorful, except for the protagonist. I suggested that the writer try using some metaphors of the senses to make the dialogue more colorful ("That leaves a bad taste in my mouth," "That really touched me"). As we discussed the character further, we talked about putting these metaphors into the subtext. We played with the idea that the character felt controlled, but was yearning to break free, which was expressed through language and gestures. As a result, the character began to deepen and become more interesting.

You can use this idea by working with the senses through language and gestures. Then think about whether this practice works better in the text, or the subtext.

EXPRESSING THE EROTIC THROUGH METAPHORS

Plenty of films are on-the-nose about the erotic. It's about sex, so they show us sex. But the erotic can be implied and layered into the subtext. Sigmund Freud provided us with many metaphors he believed were related to sex — the cigar, the pole, the circle, the jewelry box.

Guns and bullets can be metaphors for male power and male sexuality, and for female fascinations with male strength. In *Bonnie and Clyde*, the stage directions tell us that Bonnie looks at Clyde's gun "with fascination." The weapon has an immediate effect on her. She touches it in a manner almost sexual, full of repressed excitement, then she challenges him.

```
                        BONNIE
    … but you wouldn't have the gumption to use it.
```

The idea of him using "it" is tantalizing in two ways — both for him to do something daring that takes her out of her hum-drum life, and also as a sexual come-on. When Clyde comes out of the grocery store, holding a fistful of money, the directions tell us Bonnie is "turned on." It is Bonnie who makes the first sexual moves. Right after the robbery, as Clyde is driving away, "Bonnie is all over him, biting his ear, ruffling his hair, running her hands all over him — in short, making passionate love to him while he drives. The thrill of the robbery and the escape has turned her on sexually."

The excitement of the bank robbery — the spraying bullets, the secrecy and hiding out, and Bonnie's sensuality, which is present from the first image of her pouting lips and easy sexuality, all reinforce the metaphor of sexuality.

In *It's Complicated* (2009), when Jane and Jake are ready to make love, and make a move toward the bedroom, the sprinkler goes off, foreshadowing what is to come.

In *Apocalypse Now*, Playboy bunnies arrive to entertain the troops, flying in on a helicopter to a mass of excited soldiers. In the script, as they fly in, there are missiles and punji stakes around the perimeter of their arrival (phallic symbols) and lights set up in a half circle, (which could relate to several different parts of a woman's anatomy). In the film, the images have changed, but they still suggest similar metaphors. In the film, the Playboy concert takes place on a round stage built out onto the water. Across the water are a series of small boats with lights on them in the shape of large half-circles. There are large lit-up missiles lining the back of the stadium seat risers. Although consciously, we might not be thinking of the symbols, Freud and other psychologists would tell us we're thinking of them unconsciously.

The Naked Gun series often spoofs sexual metaphors. As Lt. Frank Drebin and Jane Spencer are ready to make love, the gas fire gives an extra spurt and sigh. As they make love, in another film in the series, rockets go off and fireworks show their ardor.

Some of the work of the writer involves seeing a potential sexual metaphor, and then using it to imply sexuality. Sometimes a missile is just a missile, ready to do its job. Sometimes a cigar is simply a cigar, waiting to be smoked. But the context pulls it into metaphor, moving the audience to see, or at least feel and sense, the connection.

Many years ago, I went to an art show with a female artist. As we stood in front of a series of still lifes, she turned to me and said, "That painting is so sexy." I immediately thought, "Huh?! It's a still life. What is she seeing?" When I asked her, she began to explain the painting: "Well, look at those luscious, plump, juicy plums. And they're placed right next to the cucumbers. The peaches are over there placed next to the bananas. And the pomegranates are cut open, showing off their seeds." As she gave me a tour of the painting, I began to understand what she was getting at. As I looked closer, I realized that I, too, had felt the richness and ripeness in the painting. I was feeling some layers of subtext, and as she told me more, I saw more clearly how the metaphor worked. (I also hoped that no one around us had heard our conversation!)

It's not necessary for your entire audience to be consciously thinking of the meaning. In fact, you generally don't want the audience to be thinking too much about the real meaning of the props and images, because this can pull them out of the story rather than help them become more deeply involved. Instead, you want them to feel and sense the meaning. You help them sense the subtext by learning more about what various images and props mean unconsciously. This imagery might require reading more psychology books (a little Freud can be a good thing!) It might mean reading books about interpretations of dreams, and what these images seem to mean in the collective unconscious. It might even mean putting on your bawdy hat for a few hours now and then, in order to see other possibilities in real life and glimpse what might be done with a bit of nuancing and the addition of sexual context.

A screenwriter carefully creates what images and props best convey what is really going on. As a result, a great film becomes multi-layered and cinematically rich.

EXERCISES AND QUESTIONS FOR DISCUSSION

(1) Look at a film known for its rich images (perhaps *Lawrence of Arabia* [1962], *Out of Africa* [1985], *The English Patient*). What do the various images mean? How do they serve the story and character?

(2) What props are used in your script? Can any be added to create more resonance and associations? If you need to express sexual desire in your script, think of ways to use props, set pieces, or gestures. How far off-the-nose can you get, while still getting the point across to the audience?

(3) Can you further enrich your characters by adding more metaphors to the dialogue and gestures? First put them into the text, then into the subtext.

(4) Watch several war movies, such as *Apocalypse Now*, *Platoon* (1986), *The Thin Red Line* (1998), *Casualties of War* (1989), or *Inglourious Basterds*. Are there times when the props convey more than just a utilitarian purpose, whether gun, knife, or baseball bat? Watch some detective films that use various murder weapons, such as *Basic Instinct*, *The Fugitive*, or *Body Heat* (1981). Why was that particular murder weapon chosen?

(5) Look at some films that use storms, rain, fire, etc., such as *Elmer Gantry* (1960), *Body Heat* (1981), *The Outrage* (1964), *Rain* (1932). How are these natural forces used and what do they mean?

CHAPTER SIX
CHAPTER SIX

expressing subtext through the genre

Many genres show subtext because the genre and the story itself represent more than what's on the surface. In horror films, when the monster roars and threatens to eat the hero, it's scary, it's supposed to be scary, and we're supposed to be scared. Yet, sometimes the monster threatening the people and the town, and the things that go bump in the night are meant to represent more than just the usual scary thing. They might represent childhood fears, or they may project the abnormal psychology of the seemingly normal characters, onto a monster.

EXPLORING THE SUBTEXT IN HORROR FILMS

Many horror films comment on culture. *Invasion of the Body Snatchers* (1956) is said to be about the robotic result of Communism; others say it's about the suppression of all alternative views. The Japanese Godzilla films about giant beasts implied atomic mutations and the damage from the atomic bombs during World War II. Zombie movies often are about the human compulsion to feed only on material things. Some are also about the loss of community. In *Night of the Living Dead* (1968), the mother has failed to kill her zombie daughter so the daughter kills and feeds on her mother, thus substantiating the fear that our children will consume our lives if we do not set limits. A broader interpretation looks at the consumer culture of America, and how we feed off of and contribute to that culture. *Zombie Death House* (1987) looks at the unpredictability of genetic testing, by telling the story of how the government experiments with a new virus on death row inmates. The virus mutates when one of the inmates is electrocuted and anyone who comes in contact with them become a zombie.

Vampire movies are about people who live off the lives of others. *The Thing* (1982) tells us evil can be transferred by contact and that you can never know who, or what, someone is. Each of us can turn to the Dark Side.

Little Shop of Horrors (1986) is about greed. The plant says, "Feed me," and its caretaker has to kill people to feed the mutant venus flytrap. Eventually the plant outgrows even its master and its master is its last meal.

Movies like these might seem like B movies, but they comment on our lives and our society.

EXPRESSING SUBTEXT THROUGH SPORTS MOVIES

Sports movies often are rich with subtext, partly because the game stands for the game of life, and the props used in sports can take on extra meaning, whether a basketball, ice skate, hockey stick, or golf club. Sometimes the game has high stakes for winning and losing (the boxing match in *Pulp Fiction* [1994] or *Cinderella Man* [2005]) and sometimes it's a sexual game that is fun, and partly about who's in control, such as *Bull Durham* (1988). Sometimes the game tells us a great deal about what's important in life (*Brian's Song* [1970 & 2001/TV], *Facing the Giants* [2006], *Blindside*

[2009]). Or, the game tells us something about our society. *Invictus* seems to be a movie about rugby, but it's really a movie about racism. The team stands for the society and the possibilities for a society to reconstitute itself and win.

In *The Great Santini*, Bull Meechum and his son, Ben, play what seems to be a friendly game of basketball, watched by the mother, Lil, and the sister, Mary Anne, who seem to be cheering for Ben. Soon it becomes very clear that this game is not about basketball, but about the father-son competition. During the game, the score goes back and forth with Ben coming out ahead.

> BEN
> How do you feel, Dad. You feel a little tired?...

> LILLIAN
> Don't goad him, Ben...

> BEN
> Not one of us have ever beaten you in a single game –
> Not checkers, not dominoes, not softball, nothing.

When Ben wins, Bull is furious. Mary Anne comes up to goad him, and he tells her: "Get out of here before I knock every freckle off your face."

Bull then changes the rules, telling his son he has to win by two points. Ben reminds him it's one.

> BULL
> I changed my mind. Let's go.

> LILLIAN
> You're not going to cheat the boy out of his victory.
> Come on, be a good sport.

> BULL
> Who the hell asked you anything?

He hits her with the ball.

> BULL
> Lili, you better get in the house before
> I kick your butt.

Ben walks away, and Bull begins to goad him. He calls him a "girl" and dares him to cry. But Ben finally just turns and tells his Dad, "This little girl just whipped your ass good!" Ben is breaking away and standing up to his dad, even though his dad doesn't want to give up his place to his son.

During the middle of the night, in the rain, the father practices, wanting to make sure this never happens again.

EXPRESSING SUBTEXT THROUGH COMEDY

Sometimes comedy has subtext. It might show us actions that spell danger in other films, but under the surface we read the humorous subtext and realize we're not supposed to worry.

In broad comedies, such as *Airplane!*, on the surface, all seems lost. The two pilots and navigator are deathly ill because they ate the fish, not the steak. Other passengers are either ill or panicked. The one person who can possibly fly the plane is the ex-soldier who is psychologically scarred from his flying disasters during the war and is literally sweating buckets from anxiety. There's a storm. It's simply impossible. And all the while, we in the audience are laughing. Why? Because we've clearly tuned in to the subtext of comedy. We are not just reading the text as we watch the movie. From the first shot in the film, which compares the plane going through the clouds to a shark (*Jaws*) moving through the water, we know we're supposed to laugh.

In *Dr. Strangelove* (1964), the whole world is ready to explode from a nuclear bomb, and we're laughing. We're not taking this peril seriously because the subtext is telling us not to.

In *Meet the Parents* (2000), when Gaylord "Greg" Focker mistakenly sets fire to the grounds, we don't get concerned and hope he's arrested for reckless endangerment. We respond to the subtext instead: "This guy is so much in love, he'll do anything to keep his sweetheart!" The text might look as if it spells danger, but the subtext tells us it's all meant to be in good fun.

Musical comedies often carry subtext because the musical numbers can work against the text, or can add another meaning to the text. The musical *Chicago* (2003, by Bill Condon, from the book by Bob Fosse) has as its tagline, "With the right song and dance you can get away with murder." It sets its style through musical numbers. In the court trial, the lawyer Billy Flynn, (Richard Gere) tap-dances around the truth — quite literally, and turns the court room into a literal circus, revealing what some thought all along — that lawyers do tap dance around the truth, and that courtrooms do, sometimes, become a circus.

Sometimes a detective genre is meant to make us laugh, rather than be overly concerned about our hero who is joking while bullets fly. In real life, the mishaps that happen to James Bond would cause us great concern. Although we are meant to recognize the danger, we are also meant to laugh and enjoy and be entertained by the near misses, with Bond meeting up with "Jaws," or almost falling from great heights, or the repartee that goes on in the midst of all these dangers. The repartee tells us that nothing bad will happen to our hero, in spite of the danger we see.

SUBTEXT THROUGH POLITICAL AND SOCIAL METAPHORS

Sometimes subtext is the underlying meaning that can't be expressed because of repressive cultures or situations. The subtext might be expressed in indirect ways. In the Civil War (and before), slaves escaped by singing the song "Follow the Drinking Gourd." To their masters, they were just singing; to other slaves, the song was a reference to following the North Star to set their escape route.

Sometimes the subtext is an indirect challenge to the ruling class, perhaps expressed through the art and writing of the culture. In oppressive cultures, plays or films about freedom and oppression are not allowed, so the writer disguises what is really being portrayed. During World War II, a French version of *Antigone*, based on the Greek play, played to packed houses. The German occupiers of France loved the play. So did the French. But the Germans never understood that the themes of freedom and standing up to authority were instilling a stronger resolve in the French. The underlying meaning was about far more than a young girl who wanted to give her brother a proper burial.

During World War II, Cartier designed a caged bird pin that defined how the French felt about the Nazi occupation. At the end of the war, they designed a bird coming out of a cage to freedom. The subtext would not have been lost to the French.

Hal Ashby's film *Being There* (1979), starring Peter Sellers, was a comedic look at how we worship celebrities, believing them to be wise even though their words are "gobblygook." Chauncey Gardner (Peter Sellers), a man of low I.Q., represents the celebrities and politicians who have little to say, but whose brief sound bites seem, to some, erudite and filled with wisdom – even though Chauncey's understanding of life was all learned from television. *Being There* is a comment on our culture – how willing we are to follow the superficial, as long as words are spoken with authority.

When I was in Russia shortly after the Berlin Wall came down and the Cold War had thawed, several writers told me they had learned how to get their themes across through subtext, so they couldn't be jailed for telling the truth. They felt that with the new freedoms they might be relying too much on text and losing some of the richer writing that had come about because they couldn't be direct.

Sometimes political opinions and ideas seem too on-the-nose for an audience that might be uncomfortable discussing a particular political view, so they are disguised in the context of a film. The film *Wag the Dog* (1997) seemed to be an innocent film, but actually it was a metaphor for Bush and Reagan. The book compares a made-up war against Albania to the first Gulf War, and the president is clearly meant to be George H.W. Bush. Film critic Roger Ebert compares the war against Albania in the movie to our invasion of Grenada during the Reagan administration. Both were wars with small, unknown countries, created to keep attention away from various government scandals and mishaps. Just as the president in the movie had to find a way to take the focus off his scandalous dallying with a girl (some resonance with the Clinton sex scandal), Ebert cites that the White House in the 1980s had to distract Americans from the issue of a terrorist bomb that had killed marines in Beirut. How to change the focus in both cases? Create a small war that proves the administration can flex its muscle and still win a war. Ebert goes on to say, "Barry Levinson's *Wag the Dog* cites Grenada as an example of how easy it is to whip up patriotic frenzy, and how dubious the motives sometimes are. "(footnote, Robert Ebert review of *Wag the Dog* in the Chicago Sun Times, January 2, 1998)

Instead of the military or politics, a greedy corporation might be using all its power to go up against the little guy (*Erin Brockovich* [2000], *The Insider* [1999], *Flash of Genius* [2008], *Silkwood* [1983], *Pelican Brief* [1993], *China Syndrome* [1979]). It might be the mighty nation going up against the small, poor, determined nation (substitute Germany vs. England during World War II, or Afghanistan in its many wars, or Iraq, Vietnam, or England vs. the Colonies in the Revolutionary War). The television series *Rocky and Bullwinkle* (1959-1964) was really about the Cold War between Russia and the U.S. even though it just seemed to be a cartoon.

Done comedically and satirically, a film can poke fun at serious political subjects, telling subtextually how the government spins the truth.

Many sci-fi movies, which take place on other planets, are really about our earthly life, since the other world stands in for our own and the aliens really are meant to be the bad guys (or good guys) on our own planet. Some sci-fi tells us about our fear of computers getting out of control (*2001: A Space Odyssey* [1968]), or about the stupidity of thinking a nuclear bomb will solve anything (*Dr. Strangelove*). The movie *Outlander* (2008), which takes place on a distant moon where there's mining going on, is really about social and civil justice, and values versus exploitation and a drug culture. Some films, such as *The Handmaid's Tale* (1990) and *Children of Men* (2006), show the sterility of the culture as evidenced by the inability of the women to have children. *Blade Runner* (1982), *Frankenstein* (1931, 1994, etc.), and *The Terminator* (1984, 1991, 2003, 2009) tell us about our technology gone amuck and coming back to get us.

The story line in any good sci-fi film usually intends to tell us something about our own social issues on earth, about the bad choices and mistakes we make, about the ineffective ways we relate to each other. The mighty and powerful stand for any group of people who think they can defeat others because they are mightier.

SETTING UP THE GENRE'S SUBTEXT

When a genre plays subtext, it usually does so by setting up a clear style for the film and holding to the style throughout. To pull us into the story, the style is usually set up in the first few minutes of the film. These early moments give us permission to respond in the way the director and writer want us to, whether that means laughing, chuckling, smiling, or being amused, angry, or afraid.

Sometimes a producer or director misses the subtext of the genre, which might occur because that particular genre isn't

the director's (or writer's) specialty. One of the most difficult   137
genres to set up is dark comedy, sometimes called black comedy,
which often fails. We are meant to laugh (while, perhaps, feeling
a bit guilty about laughing) in black comedy. Most of the time,
the audience has trouble understanding the tone, partly
because it's not set up clearly enough. The audience might
think they're watching a film that is simply dark, rather than
darkly comedic.

With *Prizzi's Honor* (1985, by Richard Condon and Janet Rouch
from the novel by Richard Condon), few realized that the film
was meant to be comedic. The movie begins with the gangsters
giving a child brass knuckles for his birthday, which is meant to
be humorous. The setup is there, but not strong enough for the
audience to realize it isn't watching a regular gangster movie.

Some black comedies do succeed, and succeed admirably. *Dog
Day Afternoon* (1975) opens with bank robbers coming into the
bank, carrying what looks like a box of long-stem roses. What
is really inside is a machine gun. The first laugh in the script
comes when they try to rob the first teller and she simply puts
up a sign, "Next window, please." The next laugh comes as the
bank robber has trouble getting the machine gun out of the
flower box. The director told Frank Pierson (the writer) "but
that's funny," and Frank replied, "It's meant to be." He meant
to set up the black comedy, which carries all the way through
the robbery and aftermath. The movie gains much of its humor
from the media circus that follows the robbery.

Fargo (1996) is another black comedy that establishes the
subtextual style clearly and with great success (and the Coen
Brothers are particularly good at establishing style). From the
beginning, Jerry is desperate and in way over his head trying to
have his wife kidnapped in order to get money. The style is set
by the music and by Jerry's inability to explain what he's doing
and why he's doing it to the hired hit-men, even by the words
"based on a true story," even though it wasn't.

138 The Coen Brothers garner the same effect with *Burn After Reading* (2008, by Joel Coen and Ethan Coen), showing how some rather dumb people get in way over their heads, although Linda Litzke (Frances McDormand) does get her needed face-lift and body job by the end of the film.

The text of these films seems to be, "This is dangerous! Be worried!" but the subtext tells us, "Enjoy their stupidity and their antics! Don't take this too seriously!"

EXPLORING THE METAPHORS OF *AVATAR*

One of the top-grossing films of 2009-2010 was *Avatar*, a film that shows its subtext through metaphors of the senses — visual, sound, smell, and touch. At the beginning of the film, we get Jake Sully's backstory, find out that he was injured during a war, that he was a Marine, and that he is taking his brother's place in a mission to Pandora.

The subtext begins to unfold as we see this story is really about the mighty earthlings with their machines, their technology, their hardware, their maps and plans and schematics, going up against the indigenous people of the planet, who have a spirit-bond with horses and (some) birds and some dragons, and who live in spiritual harmony with the Spirit of the Great Tree.

The subtext represents The Civilized going up against what is seemingly an uncivilized, not-quite-human race because the powerful want the territories for their ore. This greed is meant to evoke a series of associations, such as American settlers in the early 1800s seeking land in the East, Midwest, and then West and taking land away from natives, even if it meant killing them, capturing them, or relocating them to less desirable places. The theme also evokes the idea of connections — the Nav'i are connected with the Great Spirit, the animals, (although this doesn't work until they literally connect), and interconnected as a community. The earthlings are disconnected, war-like, not living in harmony.

These associations imply certain universal themes, such as racism ("those people are less than me, therefore I can exploit them"), classism ("they're not as advanced as us," or "the one who has the gold wins — and those poor people definitely don't have the gold"), ageism ("She's got wrinkles, what good is she?"), or of sexism ("Get back in the kitchen, babe!"). Themes of greed and exploitation abound, as the conquerors believe they have a right to the resources of others. In *Avatar*, we see the colonizers "going native," taking on the dress and the rituals of the Na'vi much like other colonists.

There are also themes of logic versus emotion, or the head versus the heart. The earthlings try to figure everything out down to the second, to plan, strategize, and apply all their book learning and vast experience to what they see as The Problem. They perform the head function. Meanwhile, those from the planet live by intuition, by connecting with the spirit of animals, by listening, by making heart connections and heart decisions. They are more emotional. They weep. They plead. They chant.

The rituals are meant to evoke our associations with many rituals we've seen of indigenous people, which can seem to some frightening, silly, or superstitious. These rituals are similar to African, Native American, Asian, Pagan, and Pacific Islander rituals, and are meant to evoke closeness to the earth and to the Spirit. Although they are somewhat similar to the chanting and the rituals in *King Kong* (1933, 1976), the rituals in that film were meant to be threatening, whereas the rituals in *Avatar* are meant to help us side with the more spiritual Na'vi. No discussions occur around racism, or head versus heart, or of the meaning of the rituals. These ideas are never mentioned outright, but they resonate on the subtextual level.

As in many science-fiction films, *Avatar*'s subtext lies more with the images than with the dialogue. The images from the script find full expression through art direction, cinematography, even model making. But it is possible to go through this film (or any good visual film) and look at the contents of the scenes, and ask, "What does it really mean? What are the images telling us? What are the bigger, deeper meanings beyond a story of some earthlings who want the unobtainium from the planet, which lies underneath the special tree of the Na'vi people?"

The meanings have been discussed in a number of reviews, as various people interpret what it's really about. Some critics have said it's "a critique of capitalism," others, "It's America-hating." Still others say it's really about environmentalism or how we exploit indigenous people. (footnote: from NBC News with Brian Williams, January 5, 2010) So, what's the truth? It might be all of them, especially if all the pieces fit together to create an interpretation.

The beginning scenes set the context of the earthlings on their way to the planet Pandora. The first image we might notice is the dark colors. Space is dark. The spaceship is dark. The palette of the director for the earthlings' territory is made up of grays, dark blues, black. Why? The world of the earthlings is presented to us as a confined, monochromatic, nondimensional, logical world. This is the world of the head – and there are plans, schedules to keep, time-devices that count down the seconds, small spaces, and limits to the imagination. Workers are expected to keep to the rules, follow orders, aim directly at the objective. Everything is orderly, logical, and linear.

When Jake takes on the body of his Avatar, the colors immediately change. Jake gets away from his handlers and runs, joyfully. Once more he has the use of his legs. There is color, speed, and a world without boundaries. There is rich dark dirt, rich enough for Jake to sink his toes into. There are brightly colored flowers and lush vegetation. What are the images telling us? This story is one of contrasts between rules and imagination, between limits and freedom. Even the mountains are free and free-floating.

When we enter into the true world of the planet, it is a beautiful,
wondrous world. As we venture farther into this world, we see
waterfalls, deep mountains, colorful birds, large creatures, and
trees. It is verdant, rich, and moist. Things grow here — and
grow big — the animals and the plants and the trees. It's a
dimensional world where life is bigger than rules, and bigger
than the physical space of the planet. The Na'vi's worldview includes belief in an afterlife, a deep spiritual life, and a feeling
for the sacredness of Nature and the importance of bonding
with animals and with each other.

The Na'vis are clearly meant to evoke images of indigenous,
especially Native American, people. They use arrows, some
dipped in poison. They put on war paint before battle. They
chant. They make a blood-curdling sound before riding into
battle on their horses and birds. They wear loincloths and
headdresses and they teach their ways to Jake. Jake enters into an
initiation ceremony much like Native American men learn the
ways of the elders as they are accepted into the tribe as adults.
The contrasts between the two worlds continue to be revealed,
as Jake moves back and forth between the base to the Na'vis,
until he feels the base is the dream and the verdant planet is the
reality.

Avatar also features a number of images of trust. In spite of the
danger of the deep chasms, Jake discovers he can trust the trees,
trust the leaves, trust his mentor, even trust the animals, once
he has made a connection with them.

We see spiritual images, the first being the white seedlings that
are free-floating. The image of the seed is used in a number of
religions. Jesus compared our spiritual life to a mustard seed,
which is small but grows to be one of the largest trees just like
faith and spirituality grows and develops. Seeds imply life ready
to sprout, just as Jake's life will sprout, grow, and develop.

When Naytiri would just as soon kill Jake, the seedlings flock to him, surrounding him with peace and light. Jake immediately recognizes that he has been chosen, and she must acknowledge him and allow him to live.

Mythologist Pamela Jaye Smith adds some other meanings to these seedlings:

> Beyond these spiritual metaphors, the fluffy flying seedlings in *Avatar* can well have another meaning. They seem to be sentient beings which flock to him, first in response to his supposed threat and then seem to recognize and accept him. In this sense they are like the little birds and animals of the forest around *Snow White*, the mice in *Cinderella*, and the animals around Mowgli in *The Jungle Book* — they represent Nature and its acceptance and protection of these unique strangers in their midst. This connection between animals and a hero is reflected in many myths, including those of Gilgamesh and Enkidu and Siegfried from the Ring Cycle operas. Those who can "hear and speak" with the animals are deemed special and have an added advantage over regular beings.

Later, we see three trees. Trees are also a spiritual metaphor. Genesis talks about the Tree of Life and the Tree of the Knowledge of Good and Evil. God tells Adam and Eve they can eat of any tree in the garden, including the Tree of Life, but not the Tree of the Knowledge of Good and Evil. Trees figure into the myths of many other cultures, including the world tree of Norse mythology, the sacred oaks of the Druids, the Kabalistic tree of mystical Judaism, and Buddha's Bodhi tree.

There are three trees in this story — the one binding the community together around a spiraling center, reminiscent of the DNA helix, plus two sacred trees that bind the community to its ancestors and to a spiritual center. The roots of the trees all connect with each other and communicate with each other, showing that all are part of a Tree of Life.

All three trees are life-giving and life-enhancing. Although there isn't a tree of Good and Evil per se, the conquering earthlings (such as the Colonel) represent forces out of harmony, those who have no perception of the evil they do.

There are sound metaphors such as the pounding of the animals running, (a strong physical force), the chanting of the community, (a spiritual communal force), the breathing in the transformer Pods, the war sounds, and crunching of trees during the attack.

Some of the metaphors use smell as a metaphor of connection and harmony. Naytiri smells Jake. Smell is used to show attraction and acceptance. Smell often plays a huge role in sexual courting and mating.

There are metaphors of taste. When Jake is first free as an Avatar, he picks a plant and eats it. The moist and tasty plant is a kind of food for his soul.

There are also metaphors of the spiritual life. The roots of the trees connect with each other like neurons. The Na'vis train their animals by connecting their spirit to the spirit of the animals. When Jake moves from his life as an earthling to his life as an Avatar, there is a flash of light. Light is a metaphor for The Spirit. His journey back is abrupt and is depicted by showing Jake waking up in his contained casket, once more having legs he must lift when he moves into the confined space of his wheelchair.

The afterlife is expressed as Eywa, The Great Mother, who embraces her people and does not take sides. When Grace is dying, she sees beyond the tree into the Spirit and announces, "It's real!" The spirit tree evokes many cultures that talk about the interconnectedness of all life. Another metaphor is enacted by the tendrils the Na'vi have at the end of their braids, which appear to be an extension of their brain/neurons systems and through which they make telepathic connections to the animals and each other.

There are images of community worship – as The People chant in unison to the Great Spirit, and make movements of waving their hands, standing, and sitting. Although these rituals suggest rituals of indigenous people, the ritual of the laying on of hands also takes place when Jake is accepted into the tribe; this act is somewhat reminiscent of Christian rituals at the ordination of a priest or minister, or of Christian healing rituals. Some of the movements are similar to the Kecak dance of Bali and to African circle dances. The subtext implies connections and turning inward for truth and guidance.

There are also metaphors related to wars, violence, and conquering. The General is inside the armored machine, a metaphor for the protection of the physical body, but also showing how his emotions and ethics obviously have a hard exterior. Director James Cameron evokes some of these notions by shooting the scenes in a certain way. When the community tree is destroyed and the Na'vis leave as their tree burns in the background, the image of the community walking away from the flaming village center is close to the famous image used in *Platoon*, where the Americans and the villagers leave the burning village. In both, the music of the film score evokes sadness. In *Platoon*, Samuel Barber's "Adagio for Strings" is used to evoke emotion. In *Avatar*, the film score behind this scene is primeval and almost atonal.

Some of these images are reinforced through dialogue. The earthlings are seen as subhuman and called "blue monkeys," "aborigines," and "indigenous people." When Jake first arrives, the soldiers make a snide comment about him, which shows the divisions even between the earthlings. The Na'vis call themselves "The People" and the earthlings the "Sky People." Clearly neither group understands or respects each other. The earthlings can't figure out why their gifts of education, medicine, and roads are not appreciated by the Na'vis. Jake finally tells the other earthlings they have nothing the Na'vi want, thus evoking how civilized nations believe that undeveloped nations really want more "things."

SUBTEXT: A SUMMARY   145

At its best, a great story expressed through any genre is like the island depicted on the cover of this book — evocative, provocative, suggestive, and often mysterious. With great characters and strong cinematic images, there is always more than meets the ear or the eye. With great subtext, we sense that much lies beneath.

EXERCISES AND QUESTIONS FOR DISCUSSION

(1) What's the genre of your script? Do meanings come across through the genre?

(2) Watch five horror films, or five sci-fi films. What do they tell us about the nature of our society?

(3) Watch some dark comedies such as *Pulp Fiction* (1994), *Raising Arizona* (1987), *Prizzi's Honor*, or *Fargo*. What tells you to laugh, in spite of the violence?

(4) Go through your script and look at the images and sounds you use. Are they used subtextually or just in the text? Can you make them work subtextually?

(5) Make up visual and sound metaphors for your script. Can you add metaphors of taste, smell, and touch?

CHAPTER SEVEN

Writer Alvin Sargent Ruminates about Subtext

One of my favorite films for many years has been *Ordinary People*. When I think of films with rich subtext, I often go back to that film to look at the layers, the subtleties, the complex relationships, and the small gestures that show us the world of these characters and their struggles. I asked writer Alvin Sargent if he would consent to an interview. He suggested I just let him write what comes into his mind about this subject, ruminate on it, think it through a bit, feel his way through it. I encouraged him simply to say what he wanted about how he approaches subtext, how he finds it, how he responds to it. As a writer of a broad range of films, including *Ordinary People*, *Paper Moon* (1973), and *Spiderman 2*, Sargent has played and worked extensively with subtext. He wrote the following to me:

Everything is subtext or has subtext or was subtext. I am sick of subtext and I suppose that in itself is subtext. It is everywhere and I am not interested in it when I am writing which is what I am up to these days with a story that has so many angles and changes and subways to new people and behavior and I can't think about the structure of the story.

I am not a builder of structure; it comes along by itself from out of itself; behavior and intention at work leading to consequence. That is the road to continuity. Not knowing, but moving along, as on a trip through a new part of the world always leads to action and again consequence. Sooner or later some difficulty might, hopefully, appear and the story begins to unfold. So much of it is connected to what has already taken place, the slow and sometimes not so slow creation of personalities and their behavior. Change behavior and you have interest renewed.

In the *Spiderman* films, there is more than one is ready for. That's a wonderful thing, I think. The element of surprise for the writer! There is no better friend to spend the day with. So often, and not often enough, I have been faced with a problem, a dilemma that I have no answer for, but then, of course, it isn't my problem, my dilemma — it is the character's. I like the words hung above my desk: *If you have a problem, give the problem to the character.* Wait long enough and the answer will appear. Like that baseball movie.

Story is like a piñata, break it open and subtext spills across the floor. If I concentrate on it, I will stop at every gas station along the trip. I wait and wait and when I am tired of waiting, I dive into a place I don't even understand, a room or forest where I left the characters, find a new piece of dialogue that from its own nowhere has a text of its own and I can apply it to the story I just left, a stranger showed up and is now a new part of the trip.

Ordinary People, though from a wonderful book, begins on the screenplay page with a bunch of people leaving a community theater play. We hear their conversation and learn a little, take them home and learn a little more, get introduced to characters and watch mind play. That way of working, telling the story, forces me to continue on, not looking for subtext, but I suppose it's happening if you want to call something by that name. And so the tale goes on with behavior exposing their problems. Plenty of it comes together though. Various vehicles headed for a crossroads where they will meet, connect, and hopefully explode to a larger piece of drama. Or see the fire put out and PULL BACK to see the father and son waiting for what comes next. A brief stop on the road.

Seated at the table, ready for a reading, are the actors, the director, the art director, heads of all the departments... well, not all of them... reading through the script. It can take a couple hours, but the hours continue on and the talk is deep and inquiring. Actors asking questions, needing to know more, finding subtext that the writer wasn't writing. Now I hear it and it's exciting to know how much I had created. The actors will tell me that, the director, anyone paying attention to the words, to the characters. Subtext: I didn't write that, but there it is. In our own lives, subtext. We take off our mask sometimes, as did Peter Parker in Spider-Man, and looked to see his real self... only to learn he has no way of destroying his subtext.

CHAPTER EIGHT

Afterword

In the movie *Shrek* (2001, from the book by William Steig and screenplay by Ted Elliott, Terry Rossio, Joe Stillman, Roger S.H. Schulman), Shrek says:

```
                        SHREK
        There's a lot more to ogres than people think.

          Onions have layers. Ogres have layers.
```

Shrek might have been talking about subtext. Great writing has layers, and more layers, and more layers. No word, or gesture, or action is arbitrary. Much of what is said and done in a great film implies and suggests something else — whether a contradiction, or an association, or an innuendo. The text is what we see — which is only the outside of the onion, or just the tip of the iceberg. The subtext is all the rest.

Subtext is what makes great writing feel like so much is going on. Like an exploration, great films go deeper and deeper, and become richer and richer with every viewing. It isn't just the text, it's the subtext. It's not just what's in the lines, it's what's between the lines — and everywhere else.

Filmography

2001: A Space Odyssey – a Warner Bros. Studio production, 1968

3:10 to Yuma – a Sony Pictures Ent. production, 1957; a Lionsgate production, 2007

500 Days of Summer – a 20th Century-Fox Film Studio production, 2009

A Beautiful Mind – a Universal Studio production, 2001

Airplane! – a Summit Entertainment production, 1980

All Quiet on the Western Front – a Universal Studio production, 1930

American Beauty – a Dreamworks Studio production, 1999

The Apartment – a United Artists Studio production, 1960

Apocalypse Now – a Paramount Studio production, 1979

As Good as It Gets – a Columbia/Tristar Pictures Production, 1997

Avatar – a 20th Century-Fox Film production, 2009

154

Babette's Feast – Danish Film Institute, 1987

Back to the Future – a Universal Studio production, 1985

Basic Instinct – a Tri Star Pictures Production, 1992

Being There – a Warner Bros. Studio production, 1979

The Big Sleep – a Warner Bros. Studio production, 1946

Blade Runner – a Warner Bros. Studio production, 1982

Blindside – a Warner Bros. Studio production, 2009

Body Heat – a Warner Bros. Studio production, 1981

Bonnie and Clyde – a Warner Bros. Studio production, 1967

Bound for Glory – a United Artists Studio production, 1976

Brian's Song – a Columbia-Tri Star Studio production, 1970;
        Sony Pictures production, 2001

Brideshead Revisited – a Miramax Studio production, 2008

Broadcast News – a 20th Century-Fox Film Studio production, 1987

Brokeback Mountain – a Focus Features production/
        Paramount Pictures production, 2005

Bull Durham – an MGM/UA Studio production, 1988

Burn After Reading – a Universal Studio production, 2008

Casablanca – a Warner Bros. Studio production, 1943

Casino Royale – a Pinewood Studio/MGM-UA production, 2006

Casualties of War – a Columbia/Tri-Star production, 1989

Cheers – a Paramount Television Production, CBS, 1982-1993

Fatal Attraction – a Paramount Studio production, 1987

Flash of Genius – a Universal Studio production, 2008

Frances – a Universal Studio production, 1982

Frankenstein – a Universal Studio production, 1931

The Fugitive – a Warner Bros. Studio production, 1993

Girl, Interrupted – a Columbia Pictures production, 1999

The Gladiator – a Dreamworks (USA) Universal Studio (non-USA) production, 2000

The Godfather – a Paramount Studio production, 1972

The Godfather: Part II – a Paramount Studio production, 1974

The Great Santini – a Samuel Goldwyn Studio production, 1979

High Fidelity – a Buena Vista Pictures Studio production, 2000

High Noon – a United Artists Studio production, 1952

The Hurt Locker – a Summit Entertainment production, 2008

I Never Promised You a Rose Garden – a Walt Disney Studio production, 1977

I'm Dancing As Fast As I Can – a Paramount Studio production, 1975

Inglourious Basterds – a Universal Studio production, 2009

The Insider – a Touchstone Pictures production, 1999

Invasion of the Body Snatchers – an Allied Artists Studio production, 1956

Invictus – a Warner Bros. Studio production, 2009

It's Complicated – a Universal Studio production, 2009

Jacob's Ladder – a Paramount-Tri-Star production, 1990

Jaws – a Universal Studio production, 1975

The Jungle Book – a Buena Vista Home Entertainment production, 1967

King Kong – RKO Radio Pictures, Inc., 1933

King Kong – Paramount Pictures, 1976

L.A. Confidential – a Warner Bros. Studio production, 1997

The Last Picture Show – a Columbia Tri Star Entertainment production, 1971

Lawrence of Arabia – a Sony Pictures Studio production, 1962

Little Shop of Horrors – a Warner Bros. production, 1986

Life as a House – a New Line production, 2001

Like Water for Chocolate – a Miramax Studio production, 1992

Lolita – an MGM Studio production, 1962

The Lord of the Rings – a Warner Bros. Studio production, 2001, 2002, 2003

Mad Men – a Lionsgate production, AMC Television, 2007 – present

Meet the Parents – a Universal Studio production, 2000

Member of the Wedding – a Sony Pictures Studio production, 1952

The Messenger – an Oscilloscope Laboratories production, 2009

Modern Times – a United Artists Studio production, 1936

My Fair Lady – a Columbia Pictures & CBS Films Studio production, 1964

Naked Gun Series – a Paramount Studio production, 1988, 1991, 1994

New in Town – a Universal Studio production, 2009

Night of the Living Dead – a Columbia Pictures Studio production, 1968

On the Waterfront – a Columbia Pictures Studio production, 1954

One Flew Over The Cuckoo's Nest – a Fantasy Film/UA Studio production, 1975

Ordinary People – a Paramount Studio production, 1980

Out of Africa – a Universal Studio production, 1985

Outlander – a Weinstein Co. production, 2009

The Outrage – a Metro-Goldwyn-Mayer production, 1964

Paper Moon – a Paramount Studio production, 1973

The Pelican Brief – a Warner Bros. Studio production, 1993

The Piano – an Artisan Entertainment production, 1993

Pirates of the Caribbean – a Disney Studio production, 2003, 2006, 2007

Platoon – an MGM/UA Studio production, 1986

The Picture of Dorian Gray – a Warner Bros. Studio production, 1945

Pride and Prejudice – BBC, an A & E production, 1996

Prizzi's Honor – a 20th Century-Fox Film production, 1985

Psycho – a Universal Studio production, 1960

Public Enemies – a Universal Studio production, 2009

Pulp Fiction – a Walt Disney Studio production, 1994

Raiders of the Lost Ark – a Paramount Studio production, 1981

Rain – 1932, from the stage play, *Rain*, 1923

Raising Arizona – a 20th Century-Fox Films production, 1987

The Reader – a Weinstein Co. production, 2008

The Remains of the Day – a Columbia Studio production, 1993

Revolutionary Road – a Dreamworks Studio production, 2008

Rocky and Bullwinkle – Bullwinkle Studios, TV, 1959-1964

Runaway Bride – a Paramount Studio production, 1999

Shadow of Doubt – a Sony Pictures Studio production, 1943

Shane – a Paramount Studio production, 1953

Shrek – a Dreamworks Pictures production, 2001

Shutter Island – a Paramount Studio production, 2010

Sideways – a Fox Searchlight production, 2004

The Silence of the Lambs – an MGM Studio production, 1991

Silkwood – a 20th Century-Fox Studio production, 1983

Slumdog Millionaire – a Warner Bros. Studio production, 2008

Snow White – a Walt Disney Studio production, 1937

The Soloist – a Universal Studio production, 2009

Spiderman – a Universal Studio production, 2002

Spiderman 2 – a Columbia Pictures Studio production, 2004

Sybil – a Warner Bros. Studio Production, 1976

The Terminator – a Universal Studio production, 1984, 1991, 2003, 2009

Thelma and Louise – an MGM/UA Studio production, 1967

The Three Faces of Eve – a 20th Century-Fox Film Corp. production, 1957

The Thing – a Universal Studio production, 1982

The Thin Red Line – a 20th Century-Fox Films production, 1998

To Have and Have Not – a Warner Bros. Studio production, 1944

Tom Jones – a Universal Studio production, 1963

Troy – a Warner Bros. Studio production, 2004

Up – a Pixar Studio production, 2009

Up in the Air – a Dreamworks Studio production, 2009

Valkyrie – a United Artists Studio production, 2008

Wag the Dog – a New Line Cinema production, 1997

Watcher in the Woods – a Walt Disney Studio production, 1980

Weeds – a Lionsgate TV production, 2005-present

Whale Rider – an Odeon Films production, 2002

What's Eating Gilbert Grape – a Paramount Studio production, 1993

The White Ribbon – a Sony Pictures Studio production, 2010   161

Will Success Spoil Rock Hunter? – a 20th Century-Fox Studio
                            production, 1957

Witness – a Paramount Studio production, 1985

Women in Love – a Brandywine Productions, Two Cities Films/
                  UA Studio production, 1969

Working Girl – a 20th Century-Fox Studio production, 1998

Zombie Death House – an Image Entertainment production, 1987

About The Author:

DR. LINDA SEGER began her script consulting business in 1981, based on her doctoral dissertation, "What Makes a Script Work?" Since then she has consulted on over 2000 scripts and over 100 produced films. Clients have included Peter Jackson, Ray Bradbury, William Kelley, Tony Bill, TriStar Pictures, as well as other Academy Award winners, Emmy Award winners, and winners of International Screenwriting Contests and Film Festivals. She has given seminars in 31 countries around the world, and to many companies and professional organizations, including Disney, ABC, CBS, NBC, ZDF in Germany, RAI Television in Rome, WGA, DGA, AFI, and the Motion Picture and Television Academies. She is the recipient of several awards, including the Candlelight Award from Regent University for being a light to the entertainment industry, the Redemptive Storyteller Award for Lifetime Achievement from the Redemptive Film Festival, the Living Legacy Award from the Moondance International Film Festival for her work in support of women, and the Distinguished Alumni Award from Pacific School of Religion. She is the author of twelve books, nine on screenwriting. She now lives in the Rocky Mountains of Colorado.

Her website is *www.lindaseger.com*

AND THE BEST SCREENPLAY GOES TO...
LEARNING FROM THE WINNERS
SIDEWAYS, SHAKESPEARE IN LOVE, CRASH

DR. LINDA SEGER

This book provides a CSI (Crime Scene Investigation) approach to Academy Award®-winning screenplays, giving you the nitty gritty details of how an Academy Award® script was created.

This extensive look at what makes an Academy Award®-winning screenplay is an insightful study of the details and nuances of three top scripts by one of Hollywood's most respected screenwriting gurus.

Dr. Seger's keen eye and vast experience shed light on the challenges that each screenplay had to overcome on the road to becoming an Oscar® winner. Includes unique Script Analysis and never-before-published interviews with the writers/directors who've won the big award.

"Haggis and Moresco couldn't have said it any better and they have the Academy Award. Your dissection of every plot line blending into the other is so on the money. I even picked up some nuances from you, and I've seen the film 412 times. Thanks. Every upcoming screenwriter should read this. Come to think of it, almost every screenwriter should read this."
— Mark Harris, Producer, *Crash* (Academy Award® for Best Picture)

"No study of the workings of a film script is better analyzed and better written than this. Seger is better at this than any books I've read about writing screenplays."
— Alvin Sargent, Academy Award®–Winning Screenwriter, *Ordinary People*

"We go to movies with friends so we can talk about them afterwards. Reading And the Best Screenplay *is like going to the movies with your best friend, if your best friend was the smartest person you've ever met — you come out loving the movie even more after you've heard her tell you why you loved it in the first place."*
— Ellen Sandler, former Co-Executive Producer, *Everybody Loves Raymond*
Author, *The TV Writer's Workbook*

DR. LINDA SEGER created and defined the job of script consultant when she began her business in 1981. Since then she has consulted on over 2000 scripts. Her clients include writers, producers, directors, editors, executives, production companies, and studios from six continents. She has worked or given seminars on screenwriting in 30 countries. She's the author of eight screenwriting books, including *Making a Good Script Great*.

$26.95 · 312 PAGES · ORDER NUMBER 78RLS · ISBN: 9781932907384

{ THE MYTH OF MWP }

In a dark time, a light bringer came along, leading the curious and the frustrated to clarity and empowerment. It took the well-guarded secrets out of the hands of the few and made them available to all. It spread a spirit of openness and creative freedom, and built a storehouse of knowledge dedicated to the betterment of the arts.

The essence of the Michael Wiese Productions (MWP) is empowering people who have the burning desire to express themselves creatively. We help them realize their dreams by putting the tools in their hands. We demystify the sometimes secretive worlds of screenwriting, directing, acting, producing, film financing, and other media crafts.

By doing so, we hope to bring forth a realization of 'conscious media' which we define as being positively charged, emphasizing hope and affirming positive values like trust, cooperation, self-empowerment, freedom, and love. Grounded in the deep roots of myth, it aims to be healing both for those who make the art and those who encounter it. It hopes to be transformative for people, opening doors to new possibilities and pulling back veils to reveal hidden worlds.

MWP has built a storehouse of knowledge unequaled in the world, for no other publisher has so many titles on the media arts. Please visit www.mwp.com where you will find many free resources and a 25% discount on our books. Sign up and become part of the wider creative community!

Onward and upward,

Michael Wiese
Publisher/Filmmaker